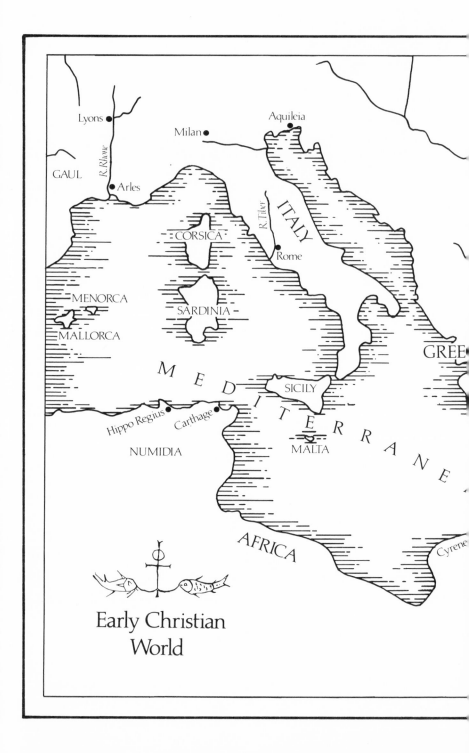

Lyons

GAUL

R. Rhone

Arles

Milan

Aquileia

ITALY

R. Tiber

Rome

CORSICA

MENORCA

MALLORCA

SARDINIA

GREE

M E D I T E R R A N E

SICILY

Hippo Regius Carthage

MALTA

NUMIDIA

A F R I C A

Cyrene

Early Christian
World

CISTERCIAN STUDIES SERIES: NUMBER ONE-HUNDRED AND NINE

A CLOUD OF WITNESSES

David N. Bell

CHRIST PANTOCRATOR. Mosaic, 1100.

CISTERCIAN STUDIES SERIES; NUMBER ONE-HUNDRED AND NINE

A CLOUD OF WITNESSES

An Introductory History
of the Development of Christian Doctrine

by

David N. Bell

Illustrations by Alice Duthie-Clark

Cistercian Publications Inc
Kalamazoo, Michigan
1989

Cistercian Publications Inc. Editorial Offices
Institute of Cistercian Studies
Western Michigan University
Kalamazoo, MI 49008
Cistercian Publications are available in Britain and Europe
from A. R. Mowbray & Co Ltd
St Thomas House Becket Street
Oxford OX1 1SJ
Elsewhere, including Canada, orders should be sent to
Cistercian Publications
St Joseph's Abbey
Spencer, MA 01562
The work of Cistercian Publications is made possible in part
through support from Western Michigan University
to the Institute of Cistercian Studies.

Library of Congress Cataloguing-in-Publication

Bell, David N., 1943–
    A cloud of witnesses : an introductory history of the development of
Christian doctrine / by David N. Bell ; illustrations by Alice Duthie-Clark.
        p.   cm.— (Cistercian studies series : no. 109)
        Includes index.
        ISBN 0–87907–609–7. — ISBN 0–87907–709–3(pbk)
    1. Theology, Doctrinal—History—Early Church, ca.30–600.
        I. Title.   II. Series
        BT25.B38   1989
        230'.09'015—dc19
        D88–32283
CIP

Printed in the United States of America.

TABLE OF CONTENTS

LION. Adapted from a fifth-century mosaic floor at Antioch.

PREFACE

T HIS LITTLE BOOK is not intended to be a substitute for such excellent volumes as J.N.D. Kelly's *Early Christian Doctrines* (1968 [fourth edition]), or the first volume of Jaroslav Pelikan's *The Christian Tradition: A History of the Development of Doctrine* (1971), or even for the old but sound survey by J.F. Bethune-Baker, *An Introduction to the Early History of Christian Doctrine* (1903). It is, instead, intended to be an introduction to such works as these, laying the foundations for their more detailed investigation, and preparing the ground for their more thorough examination. It is a book in which footnotes have been virtually eliminated, in which Greek and Latin terms have been severely curtailed, and in which the multitudinous and colourful *dramatis personae* of early Christian doctrinal history have been reduced, if not to a minimum, at least to a workable number. It is not intended for the specialist or the scholar, but simply for anyone interested in learning something about the way in which the doctrines of early Christianity developed.

It is also a book in which the discerning reader will find two different styles of writing, one colloquial and one literary; a large number of analogies drawn from everyday life; and, in some cases, what some might consider to be a somewhat impious attitude to the sacred truths of the Christian religion. Perhaps, then, one should say a word or two about these matters. Firstly, to write in a uniform style is simple, but soporific; and since many of the early fathers had little hesitation in using colloquialisms, neither have I. Secondly, some of the analogies may be thought by some to be a little earthy. But as all of us are or should be aware, the most rarefied truths may often be expressed in very earthy language. The Bible itself is sufficient witness to the principle. Thirdly, impiety, like beauty, may well be in the eye of the beholder. The views and opinions of the early fathers range, like the ideas of most of humanity, from the sublime to the ridiculous, and if some of the ideas are indeed just plain silly, it would be dishonest and misleading not to say so. The Sufi tradition rightly maintains that one cannot teach a person who has no sense of humour (few nowadays would subscribe to the view of Saint John Chrysostom that Christ never laughed), and those who have none should not read this book.

Simplification has, of course, been essential. As I said earlier, this is merely an introduction to patristic studies, not a comprehensive examination. It has not been possible, therefore, to deal with all the ramifications of, let us say, the Christological controversy and its aftermath, for not only are the political and ecclesiastical complexities themselves too difficult for a book of this nature, but a full understanding of the matter demands a working knowledge of at least Greek and Latin (and preferably Syriac and Coptic), and not everyone has this to hand. Simplification, however, is also dangerous, and if I have on occasion lapsed into over-simplification (a euphemism for inaccuracy) I am sure that my reviewers will point it out.

If this volume is found to be too brief, longer studies (such as those already noted) are easily available; and as Oliver Goldsmith said:

> Good people all, of every sort,
> Give ear unto my song;
> And if you find it wond'rous short,
> It cannot hold you long.

CONSTANTINE THE GREAT. Adapted from an early fourth-century bust.

CHAPTER I

AN HISTORICAL OUTLINE

TO UNDERSTAND AND APPRECIATE the course of Christianity and the development of Christian ideas over the first five centuries, it is essential to keep in mind certain major events and certain major dates. The history of the first centuries of Christianity may therefore be divided into five main periods, as follows: (1) To 250: The Beginnings of Persecution; (2) From 250 to 311: Systematic Persecution; (3) From 311 to 325: The Rise of Constantine; (4) From 325 to 392: The Triumph of Imperial Christianity; and (5) From 392 to the end of the fifth century: The Division of the Roman Empire. Let us glance very briefly at each of these periods in turn.

1. *The Beginnings of Persecution*

After the execution of Jesus of Nazareth, Christianity, primarily through the efforts of Paul and his followers, spread from Palestine to the gentile world of the Mediterranean. The ruler of the Mediterranean world at this time was Rome, and to a large extent, therefore, the early history of Christianity becomes a history of its dealings with the Roman administration.

The Romans, on the whole, were remarkably tolerant in the matter of religion and, with very few exceptions, left their citizens to worship whatever gods they preferred in whatever way they desired, *provided*—and it is a very important proviso—they also worshipped the Emperor. 'Worship,' however, is here an unfortunate term, for the rite itself was simple (it could demand, for example, no more than burning a pinch of incense before a statue of the Emperor) and was regarded by the majority of Roman administrators more as a political than a religious gesture. That is, it was seen as a religio-political ritual by which one indicated one's affiliation to the Roman empire and one's recognition of the Roman emperor as the legitimate ruler.

Only the Jews were exempt from this requirement, and so long as Christianity was viewed as a Jewish sect, it, too, could claim the same exemption. But as soon as Christianity saw itself, and was seen, as a separate and distinct religion, the Romans naturally required of the Christians all that they required of the other religious groups in the Empire, including the 'worship' or recognition of its legally constituted ruler. It was, for the most part, a sort of early pledge of allegiance.

This the Christians refused to do, not because they would not acknowledge the Emperor (they were, in fact, some of the most law-abiding citizens of the Empire), but because they considered the rite to be a denial of the basic Christian principle that the only object of worship could be and should be the one God. In other words, the Christians, for primarily *religious* reasons, refused to participate in a rite which, for primarily *political* reasons, was required of all by Rome.

The consequences of this were as inevitable as they were unfortunate: the Christians were suspected of treason against the state, of refusing to acknowledge the Emperor, and of denying the legitimacy of Roman authority. And in addition to this, the Christian communities in Rome and elsewhere had become generally disliked and suspected within twenty years of the death of Jesus of Nazareth. The reasons for this will be considered in detail a little later, but suffice it to say for the moment that the Christians were regarded as exclusive and secretive sectarian groups who were convinced that they were better than everyone else, and who participated in religious rituals which were, to say the least, highly suspect. It is all very well for a modern Christian to speak of 'eating the flesh' and 'drinking the blood' of Christ: everyone knows that the language is here allegorical or symbolic. But the average Roman of the first century heard the words literally and drew the obvious though mistaken conclusion that the Christians were cannibals.

The result was persecution, but until about the middle of the third century, persecution was local and sporadic. It would flare up in one city for a month or a year or more and then simmer down, only to flare up again in another city elsewhere. There were, however, two persecutions of considerable duration and violence: those of Nero (from 54 to 68) and of Trajan (from 98 to 117). Yet continual, widespread, and systematic persecution did not occur until the second half of the third century: the second period in this very brief history.

2. *Systematic Persecution*

During the later third and early fourth centuries, the Roman empire underwent a series of crises, some military, some economic, and many which were both. The internal unity of the Empire was threatened and there was general unrest and dissension. It was not difficult, in these troubled times, to see the Christians—the disliked, distrusted, secretive, exclusive Christians who refused to worship the Emperor—as being at or near the source of these very serious disorders. The Roman administration, in fact, tended to regard Christians in much the same light as the Jews were regarded in Nazi Germany, and the fact that the

Christians themselves were innocent of almost all the accusations levied against them was quite irrelevant. Then as now, it was what people believed which was important, and there is no doubt that people often believed the worst of the Christians and frequently treated them as scapegoats.

The consequences of this intensified persecution, however, were not quite what the persecutors intended. Instead of annihilating Christianity and destroying its communities, the external threat served rather to unite and bind the Christians more strongly together. And there can be no doubt that the extraordinary courage of many of the early martyrs gave hope, confidence, and encouragement to those who had not yet suffered. Under these conditions petty rivalries were forgotten and local disputes dwindled into insignificance, and there is a great deal of truth in Tertullian's famous statement that the blood of the martyrs was the seed of the Church.

The last of the great persecutions was that of the emperor Diocletian, who ruled from 284 to 305. This unpleasant period was brought to a welcome close by an important decree passed by a successor of Diocletian, the emperor Galerius (305–311), who, upon his deathbed, gave his sanction to the *Edict of Toleration*. He did so, not out of love for the Christians (whom he hated) or from admiration for the faith (which he despised), but for reasons utilitarian and political. Faced with the threat of an alliance between two rival claimants to the imperial throne, Galerius found it politically expedient to conciliate the Christians, and not the least of the reasons for this conciliatory move was that one of these two rival claimants was the remarkable and charismatic Constantine.

3. *The Rise of Constantine*

Constantine (274– or 288–377) had seen service both at the court of Diocletian and with the Roman army in England, and in the year 306 was proclaimed *imperator* or 'emperor' at York. His claim to the purple, however, was not uncontested. Only in 312, just after the death of Galerius, did he defeat his rival, Maxentius, at the famous battle of the Milvian Bridge and achieve his ambition to be senior ruler of the Roman Empire.

Constantine saw clearly the political advantage of having the Christians with him rather than against him, and he was determined to bind together the secular state and the Christian church by the strongest possible ties. In 313, therefore, he reinforced the Edict of Toleration passed by Galerius with the so-called *Edict of Milan*—the precise nature and legal status of these 'edicts' need not concern us— which declared that all religions, including Christianity, were to be tolerated equally, and recognized the full legal existence of the Christian churches.

The question whether Constantine himself was truly a Christian is difficult to answer. He obviously (and wisely) preferred to have a foot in the pagan camp as well as the Christian, and although he was baptized into the Christian faith just before his death, there is no doubt that his Christianity sat but lightly on his shoulders. Nor did his conduct in later life (which included the murder of his son and his nephew) accord particularly well with the ethical principles of the New Testament.

On the other hand, he certainly admired Christianity and was certainly influenced by it. Under Constantine there was a humanization of the criminal law, an amelioration in the position of slaves, improvements in the situation of the poor, and a considerable number of benefits accorded to the Christian churches and clergy. It was Constantine, too, who, in 321, commanded that Sunday (the 'Sun-day' and the 'Son-day', with typical Constantinean ambivalence) should be a public holiday, and it was also Constantine who determined that his newly-won Empire should have a new imperial seat: the city of Constantinople (the name means 'Constantine's City'), later to become Istanbul.

With Constantine's protection and encouragement, therefore, Christianity flourished, but the consequences were not wholly fortunate. Now that the external threat had been removed, the Christians could devote themselves to what was clearly becoming their predominant interest: arguing and disputing among themselves on a multitude of theological points—some minor, some major. Undoubtedly the most important quarrel to arise concerned the doctrine of the Trinity. The causes of this great controversy, the points at issue, and its ultimate resolution we shall consider in due course, but for our immediate purposes we need only note that the disagreements (disagreements, primarily, about the place occupied by God the Son in relation to God the Father) were sufficiently deep and sufficiently intense to split the Church into two warring camps and threaten Constantine's newly-gained Empire with major civil discord.

Something, obviously, had to be done, and done with all possible speed. So Constantine called a council, a council which would be attended (at least in theory) by representatives from the whole Christian world and which would be held under his watchful eye at Nicaea (now the town of Isnik in modern Turkey, not far from Istanbul) in the early summer of the year 325. This was the First General or Ecumenical Council (the term 'ecumenical' derives from a Greek word meaning 'the civilized world'), and we shall see its full significance later.

4. *The Triumph of Imperial Christianity*

The decades following the Council of Nicaea were marked by continuing theological discord, and it took some fifty years before the tensions aroused by this first great dispute finally subsided. But these years were marked by the rapid consolidation of Christianity and the corresponding diminution in the importance and influence of paganism. The efforts of the Emperor Julian—called by the Christians Julian the Apostate—who in his short reign (361–363) attempted to reintroduce the pagan cults and degrade, if not extirpate, Christianity, utterly failed to stem the irresistible tide, and the story that Julian died with the words 'Vicisti Galilaee' ('Thou hast conquered, Galilean') on his lips, whilst historically inaccurate, is a fair reflection of the course of events. The matter came to a head in the year 392, when the emperor Theodosius I made the teaching of heresy a legal offence, outlawed paganism, prohibited sacrifice, and, to all intents and purposes, established Christianity as the only legal religion of the Roman Empire.

The consequences of this momentous decision were not altogether favourable. Many who had never had either the taste or the inclination for orthodox Christianity now 'discovered' that in their hearts they had been Christian all the time. The Christian church and the Christian state, which had been converging since the time of Constantine, now became virtually indistinguishable. Bishops became high dignitaries of state with magisterial functions; the Church acquired immense riches and huge tracts of lands; the churches themselves grew larger and larger, and more and more splendid, and hand-in-hand with this ever-increasing magnificence, the liturgy became more protracted, more complex, more elaborate, and more beautiful. Inevitably, however, this increase in wealth and power produced a corresponding increase in corruption, and despite a number of truly saintly figures, the church of the fourth century was a hotbed of intrigue, political machination, dispute, and disagreement. Some would say, in fact, that the two worst things that happened to Christianity during its first four hundred years were the end of active persecution and the elevation of the religion to the position of the official state cult.

5. *The Division of the Roman Empire*

The Christian empire of Theodosius I was no longer an harmonious and united whole. Since the time of

Constantine—indeed, for some years before his reign—the huge geographical mass of the Roman world had been dividing itself in two. Cultural, linguistic, and political differences instituted a process which led eventually to an Eastern Roman Empire, with Greek as its official language and Constantinople its capital, encompassing Greece, Asia Minor (i.e., modern Turkey), Syria, Palestine, Egypt, and the whole eastern half of the Mediterranean; and a Western Roman Empire, with Latin as its official language and its capital at Rome, encompassing Italy, North Africa, Spain, Gaul, Germany, and Britain.

This division was accentuated in the fifth century by a series of invasions by barbarian tribes—Goths, Huns, Vandals, and the like—who overran much of Europe, including Italy, during this period. Some of them were at least nominally Christian; many, including the ferocious Huns under their leader Attila, were not. But whether Christian or pagan the invaders brought on the economic and political collapse of the western half of the Empire, and the elevation to a position of major importance of the bishops of Rome.

Up to the time of Constantine, the power of the papacy had been very limited; but with the ever-increasing importance of Christianity and, most especially, the barbarian invasions of the fifth century, papal power increased enormously. The popes were seen as firm rocks in a political and social quicksand and presented to the western eye one of the few stable and, so it would appear, enduring institutions in conditions which all too frequently approached anarchy. And the popes themselves, whether they liked it or not (some of them did; some did not), were forced to extend their jurisdiction from the realm of the ecclesiastical to that of the secular. One thing is certain: from the middle of the fifth century onwards, the papacy could not be ignored, and from the time of Leo the Great (who died in 461), the Roman see, fully consolidated, enjoyed enormous prestige, influence, and importance.

The situation in the Greek-speaking east was strikingly different. With the exception of an early incursion by the Goths, the barbarian invasions generally petered out at the borders of Greece, and the eastern Roman empire, with its imperial seat in Constantinople, was not subjected to prolonged and catastrophic change until the rise of Muslim power in the seventh and eighth centuries. In the relative security of the Christian east, the theological disputes which were so congenial to the Greek mind flourished and blossomed with remarkable vigour. Paramount among the disputes was no longer the question of the Trinity—that had been settled by about 380—but the question of the person of Christ: more precisely, the question of how the divine and human parts of this unique being were united or conjoined in Jesus of Nazareth. It was this dispute— more complex and yet more bitter than that over the Trinity—which led the Emperor of the time, like Constantine before him, to call a council (or more accurately a series of councils) to attempt to settle the issue. The end result of these endeavours was the great Council of Chalcedon, the Fourth Ecumenical Council, which met in Chalcedon (almost opposite Constantinople on the other shore of the Bosphorus) on 8 October 451 and which, like the Council of Nicaea, we shall examine in detail in due course.

What happened in east and west after the fifth century need not for the moment concern us. If we bear in mind the dates of the 'edicts of toleration', of the Council of Nicaea, of the establishment of Christianity as the official religion of the Roman Empire, and of the Council of Chalcedon, we shall find this an adequate basis for the discussions to follow. Let us now, therefore, turn from history to philosophy and examine the intellectual background against which Christian doctrine developed.

THE PHILOSOPHER PLOTINUS. Adapted from a third-century roman sarcophagus.

CHAPTER II

THE INTELLECTUAL
BACKGROUND

THE IMMEDIATE DISCIPLES of Jesus of Nazareth were, of
course, converts: converts from Judaism. Similarly,
the earliest Christians to appear in the gentile world
were also converts: converts, in this case, from one or other
of the rich diversity of religions with which the Graeco-
Roman world was adequately stocked. But with any convert, it is as important—perhaps more important—to
understand what they converted *from* as what they converted *to*; for any person moving from one tradition to
another will understand and interpret the concepts of the
latter by the familiar intellectual suppositions of the former. It is essential, therefore, to appreciate the way in
which these early converts thought, for it was they who
were to become the presbyters and bishops of the Christian
churches, and it was they who were responsible for the
creation of Christian doctrine.

We need not here concern ourselves with every mode of
thought to be found within the wide reaches of the Roman
empire, but only with three: the philosophies of Stoicism
and Platonism, and that curious and eclectic collection of

loosely connected sects generally known as Gnosticism. Let us begin with Stoicism.

1. *Stoicism*

This was the school of thought founded at Athens in the fourth century bce by Zeno of Citium (335–263 bce). Its viewpoint was entirely materialistic—that is, unlike Platonism (and later, Christianity), it denied any separate world of 'spirit' and maintained that there existed only matter. Even its concept of God was not of a Supreme Being, spiritual and immaterial, but only of a more refined and subtle form of matter, a sort of formless gaseous fire which permeated all things as water permeates a sponge or light permeates the air. Yet this 'gaseous fire' was also rational and intelligent: it was not only immanent in all things, bound them together, and made them what they were, but it also ordered them in their courses and directed them to their proper ends. Because of this all-pervading 'spirit' or 'god', the law of nature and the law of duty are incumbent upon all things. For this reason puppies turn into dogs, and not into cats or jelly-fish, the seasons follow one another in their apportioned round, and seeds produce plants which produce fruit which, in turn, produce further seeds. And as for human beings: the ideal way for them is also to 'live according to rational nature', and by this the Stoics understood that the entirety of one's life would be governed by reason (not emotion) and that 'rational action' was the only proper action for a rational being. If we consider how often we act by emotion, by instinct, by desire, by lust, by greed (and one need only watch a single episode of the daily soaps to see all this), then we may appreciate a little more clearly how difficult to achieve was the Stoic goal.

Stoic influence on Christianity was confined to two main areas: firstly, the idea that all human beings are rational and have within them the 'spark of reason' or the 'divine spark'; and secondly, Stoicism had a considerable impact on the development of Christian ethics. But despite the fact that Stoic traces can be clearly discerned in the ideas of a number of theologians of the first three centuries, it was Platonism which had a far more profound effect on the making of Christian doctrine, and it is to a consideration of that school of thought to which we may now turn.

2. Platonism

Like Stoicism, this school was founded at Athens in the fourth century bce, and in the course of its development from the time of Plato (427–347 bce) to the time of the Christians it underwent a considerable number of changes. If this were a history of philosophy we would have to distinguish Middle Platonism from Neo-Platonism, but since it is not, and since our interests are not in Platonism itself but in its impact on Christianity, we can try to combine the two together and point out the main features of what we may term simply 'Later Platonism'.

The Platonists, unlike the Stoics, had no doubts of the existence of a spiritual realm, and their main concern was to explain, or to try to explain, how this spiritual realm, which was pure, unsullied, and utterly perfect, could possibly be related to this obviously imperfect, grubby, impure, unpleasant, polluted, and war-torn world. To appreciate their solution it may help if we imagine a set of traffic signals with the road underneath. Corresponding to the red light at the top was the Source of All Things, which the Platonists referred to as The One. This 'One' was there from the beginning: it has no body, no shape, no form, no passions, no needs, no desires. It is simply a 'One-ness', existing eternally, and containing within itself the potentiality for all things. If we may use a human analogy, it corresponds to a creative artist—let us say a potter—in deep sleep. He or she has the *potential* to create all sorts of things—plates, cups, vases—but at the moment is not doing anything about it. Before anything is actually created, therefore, we must move on to another stage.

This second stage is the amber light of the traffic signal, and it corresponds to our artist waking up and thinking 'I shall make a Cup'. In other words, we have now moved from the realm of *potentiality* to the realm of *thought*, but only to the realm of *abstract* thought. That is to say, the artist has simply conceived the idea of 'Cup' and has not thought of any particular cup of a specific shape and a specific size. This second stage of the process was called by the Platonists 'The Divine Mind', and whereas the first stage could be called 'The Infinite Potentiality of God', this second stage could be termed 'God thinking'. It is at this stage that the One conceives the plan of creation: it thinks 'Cup', 'Cat', 'Dog', 'Truth', 'Justice', 'Tree', and so on. But as we noted earlier, these ideas (and the Divine Mind is often referred to as The World of the Ideas) are still abstract, and although the One has now thought 'Dog', there is still a long way to go before we find a specific German Shepherd or a Cocker Spaniel running around in search of a fire hydrant.

We must therefore move on to a third stage: the green light on the traffic signal. This stage, to which the Platonists gave the curious title of The World-Soul (for reasons which need not concern us in the least), corresponds to the artist, who has already thought 'Cup', now determining exactly what sort of cup will be made. We are here concerned with the precise colour, shape, size, and material of the object and have moved from the realm of the *abstract* to the realm of the *concrete* or the *particular*. At this stage of the process, the One is thinking not just of 'Dog', but of all the different varieties of dog; not just of 'Truth', but of all its multitudinous manifestations. And when these particular and specific thoughts are merged with matter, then we have the world as we see it (this is the road beneath the green light), full of all sorts of things, all sorts of people, all sorts of animals, and all sorts of ideas. The Platonic scheme, therefore, looks something like this:

Potentiality for Dogs (and All Else)	The One	The Realm of Infinite Potentiality
The abstract idea of 'Dog'	The Divine Mind	The Realm of the Divine Ideas
The specific idea of Spaniels	The World-Soul	The Realm of Specific Ideas
A specific brown-and-white male spaniel called 'Jack'	The World	The Realm of Specific Things

Only two final points need be made with regard to this scheme: the first is that just as in the set of traffic signals the green is below the amber and the amber below the red, so, too, in Platonism, the second principle, the Divine Mind, is lower than and subordinate to the One, and the World-Soul is lower than and subordinate to the Divine Mind. Secondly, every human being is comprised of soul and body, and since the soul is a *spiritual*, not a material, entity, its true home is not here in this material world, but in the spiritual world of the Divine Mind. The soul, therefore, which is, in essence, something pure and perfect, has 'fallen' in some way from its true home and has become enmeshed or imprisoned or entombed in flesh and matter. One of the most famous sayings of the Platonists was 'The body is a tomb' (*ho sōma sēma*: the phrase sounds better in Greek), indicating the way in which they viewed the plight of humanity, and seeing the soul (if we may change the metaphor) as a bird in a cage, waiting only for the door to be opened before it can fly free, soaring up and up, alone to the Alone, back to the perfection and purity from which it came.

3. *Gnosticism*

The third of the three schools of thought we shall consider is Gnosticism, and it would be well to appreciate from the beginning that the term does not refer to one specific school alone, but to a whole collection of sectarian groups, frequently mutually antagonistic, which differed dramatically from each other in the details of their beliefs. Some are impressive; some are suspect; some are quite insane; but despite their manifold differences all were agreed upon three basic points.

Firstly, they were all Platonic in the sense that they all saw this imperfect world as being separated from the Supreme Being by a series of intermediaries. In the number and nature of these intermediaries, however, there were radical differences of opinion: some (like the Platonists) maintained there were but few; others (like the extraordinary Basilides) held that there were three hundred sixty-five of them. But however many there were, they all had their own names and characteristics, and for reasons which will become clear in a moment, these names were of the utmost importance.

Secondly, they were all Platonic in the sense that they all saw the human soul as being a perfect—or at least a moderately perfect—entity entrapped and entombed in flesh. And all were agreed that it had to be released from its prison and directed back to its true home. As to how this was to be done, the various groups were, again, at odds. Most people, of course, were quite unaware that they were 'souls imprisoned'—the Gnostics called these unfortunates 'sleep-walkers' and included by the term almost everyone who was not a Gnostic—but even if these sleepers could be roused from their somnambulant condition, further difficulties awaited them. For the various intermediaries (the Gnostics referred to them as *Aeons*) would, if possible, try to prevent the soul from returning to its source, and unless each *aeon* could be controlled and overcome, the soul would never achieve its goal. The situation can be likened to a Jacob's ladder, set between earth and heaven, with each of its dozens of rungs being guarded by an antagonistic and/or malignant being. How, then, could these *aeons* be controlled? The answer was simple: by knowing their names. Knowledge of their names gave one total power over them, and the various sects therefore entrusted to their members, under terms of the utmost secrecy, the true spellings and sounds of these appellations. That none of the various groups agreed with each other as to the nature of these names or their number need not here concern us and should cause us no surprise. But how were these names revealed in the beginning? Who taught the Gnostic teachers what they needed to know? The answer to this question leads us to the third and final point we need to consider.

Thirdly, all the Gnostic groups were agreed that redemption was a possibility—that it was possible for us to 'wake up', free our souls from our bodies, and negotiate successfully the perilous path which leads to our spiritual home—and that at certain times there had appeared redeemers who had revealed to us all the information that was necessary. The identity of these redeemers differed, as we might expect, according to the sect concerned: some, for example, suggested Simon Magus (the magician of Acts 8); some preferred Hercules; but a considerable number, though by no means all, viewed the redeemer as Jesus Christ. Christ had appeared on earth and revealed to the ignorant faithful, to the 'ordinary' Christians, the truths in the four gospels, but these truths were no more than the pabulum of the nursery. To the Gnostics he had revealed far more—the true meat of the doctrine, suitable for adults endowed with reason and courage—and the Gnostics could produce a large number of non-canonical Gospels and similar treatises to prove it. *This* was what Christ had really taught; *this* was the true Christianity; not a system which asked only simple faith, but a system which demanded intellectual understanding and secret knowledge; a system not for the many, but for the few; a system not for sleep-walkers, but for spiritual athletes; a system not for believers, but for *knowers*. And 'knower' is what 'Gnostic' means: they knew the history of creation, they knew why we are as we are, they knew the nature of the prison, they knew the way out, and they knew the pass-words which would open all doors. They knew, in short, the way home and how to get there. And there is no doubt that their knowledge was much esteemed and that Gnosticism was very popular. There is no doubt, too, that it was both feared and disliked by the Fathers of the Church.

One of the reasons for this dislike certainly entailed numbers. Early Christianity was eager to proselytise, but the pseudo-Christian Gnostic sects could frequently offer a religious system which was decidedly more attractive and far more intellectually stimulating than early Christianity; they could offer a guaranteed way to salvation; they were often much more similar to the pagan systems from which the converts were changing; and they could combine all this with the idea of a 'secret' knowledge, known only to the elect, and therefore provide their adherents with that sense of superiority, of being so much better than one's fellows, which human beings of all ages have found so dangerously attractive. If, then, pagans who were dissatisfied with the prevailing systems were looking elsewhere, there was a very good chance that when faced with a choice between 'Gnostic' Christianity and 'orthodox' Christianity, they would choose the former, and in this way (so far as the 'orthodox' were concerned) the converts would deprive themselves of the hope of salvation and the 'true' church of the advantage of numbers.

For this, and for other reasons, the Christian pastors of the first two centuries were forced to keep a continual eye— two eyes, at some times and in some places—on the progress of Gnosticism, and until it faded away in the course of the third century, it was regarded by the Church fathers as one of the greatest, if not the greatest, danger to the truth of the faith.

Of these three schools of thought—Stoicism, Platonism, and Gnosticism—it was unquestionably the second which had the most profound impact on Christian doctrine. Stoicism, as we have remarked, certainly affected Christian ethics and certain aspects of what we might call Christian psychology; Gnosticism was a threat, a rival, rather than an influence; but Platonism formed and moulded the most fundamental and distinctive principle of Christian belief: the doctrine of the Trinity; and to see how and why this occurred we must now turn our attention away from the philosophers and the Gnostics to the early Christian fathers themselves.

CHRISTIANITY SEEN BY A PAGAN. 'Alexander worshiping his God', adapted from second-century graffito.

CHAPTER III

THE APOSTOLIC FATHERS
AND THE DEFENDERS
OF THE FAITH

THE FIRST CHRISTIAN WRITERS to engage our attention are two groups of people who ranged in time from the later years of the first century to the end of the second. One group, the Apostolic Fathers, were Christians writing to Christians; the other group, the Apologists, were Christians writing to non-Christians. Because of this difference, what they have to say and the way in which they say it are quite distinct. Let us glance at the Apostolic Fathers first.

This name has been given since the later part of the seventeenth century to a group of writers who include Clement of Rome, Ignatius of Antioch, Polycarp of Smyrna, Hermas, Papias, and three or four others who have left us written records, but whose precise names and identities are obscure. They were called 'apostolic' either because they were in immediate contact with the apostles themselves, or because they received instruction from their disciples. The letters they wrote are in many ways very similar to the letters we find in the New Testament (indeed, some of their writings were considered to be part of the canon by certain churches at certain times), and, like many letter-writers, they addressed specific problems which had developed at specific places at specific times.

Clement of Rome, for example, the third successor of St Peter, writes to the church at Corinth to try to resolve a most unpleasant dispute which had led to the deposition of a number of presbyters. Bring them back, he says, and repent! God requires due and proper order in all things, and legitimate authority must be obeyed! And apart from providing us with some very valuable insights into the structure and operations of the Christian ministry of his time, Clement's letter is the earliest example we have of the intervention of the Church of Rome into the affairs of the church of another city.

Ignatius, the highly-strung bishop of Antioch, became caught up in the persecution of Trajan and, to his great delight (for he was unnaturally eager for martyrdom), was condemned to die in Rome and was led from his home city to the capital under a guard of ten soldiers. On the way he wrote a number of letters to various churches (including one to Rome in which he beseeches the Roman Christians not to intervene with the pagan administration and deprive him of his martyrdom), and in these writings we see a deep concern with the reality of the Incarnation (Christ was true God and true man, says Ignatius; he was truly born, truly suffered, truly died, and truly redeemed us) and also with the unity of the Church, which, as we know, was being threatened by persecution. How can this unity be best assured? Look to the bishop, says Ignatius! There is one church, one eucharist, one sanctuary, one faith, one bishop. Look to him; give heed to him; follow him; obey him. Without him, there shall be no baptism; without him, no eucharist. 'But what he approves, that is also

---

[1]Ignatius, *Letter to the Smyrnaeans,* 8.

well-pleasing to God.'[1] These ideas of Ignatius were important in the development of the so-called monarchical episcopate—the principle that a local church should be governed by a single bishop in whom all authority is vested—and his views on the person of Christ we shall refer to again a little later.

But for all their importance in their own time and place, these Apostolic Fathers were not systematic theologians. Indeed, whether we may refer to them as 'theologians' at all is a point which may be debated. And although they were not without significance in such areas as we have outlined above, their contribution to what are undoubtedly the two fundamental doctrines of the Christian tradition— the doctrine of the Trinity and the doctrine of the Person of Christ—was very limited. On these matters they had little to say, and what they did have to say (I am thinking particularly of Hermas) was sometimes decidedly suspect. To witness the first real developments in Trinitarian thought we must move on to the Apologists, for it was they, speaking not to a Christian but to a pagan world, who found it necessary to explain in some detail concepts which the Apostolic Fathers, Christians writing to Christians, could simply assume.

First of all, the term 'apology' is not used here in the sense in which we use it today. It meant (and means) in Greek a 'defence', and the Apologists, therefore, were not saying they were sorry to be Christian, but were defending the faith against popular pagan misunderstandings, Jewish objections, and the Gnostic threat. The Apologists, of whom there were about a dozen, flourished between about 120 ce and 220 ce, and whereas one or two were Westerners and wrote in Latin (the most important of these was Tertullian, whose ideas we shall consider later), the majority were Greeks. Of these, two are of particular note: Justin Martyr and Irenaeus of Lyons; and we shall confine our examination of the Apologists to these two major figures.

Justin was born of pagan parents at the very beginning of
the second century, and being possessed of an inquiring
mind he worked his way through Stoicism, Aristotelia-
nism, Pythagoreanism, and Platonism, before finding his
way to Christianity when he was about thirty. He then
taught in Ephesus and in Rome, and it was there, in about
165, that he and six of his disciples were arraigned before
the pagan authorities as Christians. When ordered to sacrifice, and thereby demonstrate their allegiance, to the
Emperor, they all refused, and they were accordingly
scourged and beheaded.

Justin, like the other Apologists, was concerned with
defending Christianity against popular misunderstandings. What misunderstandings? Firstly, the idea that because Christians refused to 'worship' the Emperor they
were a danger to the state (we saw how this developed in
Chapter I); secondly, that they were guilty of cannibalism
(this, too, we noted in Chapter I); thirdly, that they in-
dulged in father-daughter incest (this arose because the
early Christian eucharist was called an *agapē*, a Greek word
which means literally 'love-feast', and from the earliest
times, bishops were referred to as 'father'; if you, as a
pagan, heard that someone was going to a love-feast with
her father, what would you think?); and fourthly, that
Christianity, which apparently worshipped a legally executed criminal, was simply superstitious nonsense.

The first three of these misunderstandings were not
difficult to counter. The Christians could demonstrate with
ease that they were actually some of the most law-abiding
citizens of the empire; that when they spoke of the body
and blood of Christ, this was not to be taken quite literally;
and that a 'love-feast', despite the name (and despite the
practices of certain Gnostic sects which turned it into an
orgy), was actually a gathering of moral and high-minded
Christians in mutual charity, and not a lascivious get-
together of libidinous perverts with full-frontal nudity and
exotic sex. We might add, however, that the efforts of the

Apologists had only limited usefulness; not because what they wrote was unpersuasive (though reading the rambling prose of Justin is no easy task), but because it is unlikely that many people—particularly those in high places—ever bothered to read it. Justin himself was beheaded in about 165, and persecution was to continue for another century and a half.

The fourth accusation (Jewish as well as pagan) was more difficult to deal with. Paul had stated the case long before: 'We preach Christ crucified', he wrote in his letter to the Corinthians, 'a stumbling-block to the Jews and a folly to the Gentiles' (1 Cor 1:23). A stumbling-block and a folly it remained. The Apologists, therefore, did two things: on the one hand they tried to show that the pagan myths were very often even more stupid and foolish than the Christian narrative (which was not a particularly successful approach), and on the other (which was more positive), they attempted to explain their understanding of Christ. This, inevitably, involved explaining his relationship to the Supreme Being, or, in Christian terms, to God the Father.

Now as we observed earlier, Justin was a convert to Christianity, and the last system to captivate him before his final conversion and baptism had been Later Platonism. It was therefore natural for him to use his Platonism to explain and interpret his Christianity, and, like all other converts from this system, he found that the traffic-signal scheme of the Platonists was ready-made for Christian reinterpretation. The One becomes God the Father; the Divine Mind becomes God the Son; and the World-Soul becomes the Holy Spirit. And although there was some doubt about the third of these equations (the early Christians were even more vague on the Holy Spirit than were the Platonists on the question of the World-Soul), the first two were clear as day. Unfortunately, however, the Platonic scheme was also a subordinationist scheme—that is, the Divine Mind was subordinate and inferior to the One,

and the World-Soul subordinate and inferior to the Divine
Mind—and when Justin applied this scheme to the Christian Trinity, he opened the way to the inevitable result:
God the Son was seen as subordinate and inferior to God
the Father. Justin himself states that God the Son is 'second in order', and that the Holy Spirit occupies the third
place. But in Justin's time, and for a long period afterwards, no one realized the theological dangers which
lurked in this concept.

Platonism, then, imposed upon Christian trinitarianism
a subordinationist tendency which proved extremely tena-
cious. But what right had Justin to use the scheme at all?
Platonism, after all, was a wholly pagan system, so how
could a Christian convert like Justin defend his use of it?
Why should Christianity be interpreted by means of paganism? Justin himself realized the importance of this question, and his answer to it is one of his few original
contributions to early Christian theology.

The reason, he says, is because the Platonists and other
philosophers, together with the Jews, had received their
inspiration from Christ. Not, in this case, from Christ *after*
his incarnation, but from Christ *before* his incarnation, from
Christ the second person of the Trinity, God the Son, who
(as St John pointed out) was with the Father in the beginning (Jn 1:2). In other words, God the Son, before he was
born of Mary, implanted in the minds of certain individuals
seeds of the truth, and as these seeds blossomed and came
to fruition, those who had been inspired communicated
the truths they had received to the people of their place and
time. Plato was one such individual in whose mind such
seeds had been planted, and so, too, were the prophets of
the Old Testament. And what this meant was that Justin
did not see three separate sources of inspiration when
confronted with three books—the Dialogues of Plato, the
Old Testament of the Jews, and the New Testament of the
Christians—but one and the same source: God the Son,
who, as he himself said, was the Truth (Jn 14:6). Justin

would even go so far as to call those who had been inspired
in this way 'Christians before Christ', thus making it clear
that they had taught the truth even before the Truth itself
had become incarnate in the person of Jesus of Nazareth.
Since, therefore, both Platonism and Judaism had been
inspired by God the Son, there was no reason at all why
these 'pre-incarnational Christian' writings should not be
used to elaborate and explain 'post-incarnational Christian' writings. Later theologians were to give this thesis
the curious title of the doctrine of the *spermatic Logos*,
because (a) *Logos*, a Greek word meaning 'word' or 'reason', was the standard term used by theologians of the
period to refer to God the Son (it is a splendidly eclectic
word, being Platonic, Stoic, and, of course, Christian: 'In
the beginning was the Word [*Logos*]' (Jn 1:1), and (b) *sperma*
is the Greek word for 'seed': i.e. the 'seeds of truth' which
these early pre-christian Christians possessed led the way
to the Gospels.

Justin's doctrine of the *Logos*, therefore, is undoubtedly a
positive one, but on the matter of the third person of the
Trinity, the Holy Spirit, his views are woolly and vague.
On the other hand, we cannot really blame him for this,
since the views of everyone else were equally vague. Justin
certainly realized that one of the most important functions
of the Holy Spirit lay in the inspiration of the prophets, but
there is no doubt that he was a little unclear about the
overall role of this curious being, who is mentioned in
Scripture but never clearly identified, and there is a tendency in his thinking to confuse the functions of Son and
Holy Spirit. Irenaeus of Lyons, the last person we shall
consider in this chapter, is somewhat clearer on the matter,
but the doctrine of the Holy Spirit would not find an even
partial resolution for another two centuries, and the main
interest of these second- and third-century theologians was
unquestionably in the relationship of the Father and the
Son. And as we shall see, this alone was quite sufficiently
problematical.

Little is known of the life of Irenaeus. He was born sometime in the middle of the second century, probably in Smyrna, and was trained in Rome. From there, for reasons unknown, he made his way to Lyons, in what is now France, where he clearly established himself as an important and respected presbyter. He succeeded Photinus (who had died a martyr) in about 178, but after this he gradually becomes more and more obscure, and his last years are shrouded in mystery. Even the date of his death is unknown.

The interests of Irenaeus were markedly different from those of Justin. Whereas Justin had been primarily concerned with the pagans and the Jews, Irenaeus was primarily concerned with the Gnostics, and this, from the start, demanded a distinct approach. It will be remembered that although the Gnostics shared certain basic convictions, they disagreed with each other on practically everything else; and it will also be remembered that a number of the sects (particularly the influential Valentinians) had no hesitation in adding a number of other gospels to those of Matthew, Mark, Luke, and John, and maintained that these apocryphal gospels contained truths too meaty for the child-like palates of the uninitiated. As a consequence of this, Irenaeus realized the great importance of having an authoritative list of books which alone would be considered canonical and which would be accepted without question by all the churches. He therefore specified which books these should be (and his New Testament is almost identical to that contained in the modern Bible) and defended his choice by rational arguments. Furthermore, he goes on, these books contain teachings handed down from the earliest times, teaching transmitted from the apostles to the bishops, who were the successors of the apostles, and thence to the faithful of all the churches. 'The tradition of the Apostles which is made manifest in the whole world can be observed in every church by all who wish to see the truth.'[2] Thus, to the absurdities and disagreements of the Gnostics Irenaeus could oppose the monolithic Church, one and holy, agreed on its canon and on the nature, order, and succession of its Apostolic Tradition. The fact that the church was not entirely one, not entirely holy, and that the content of the canon would not finally be defined until the fourth century need not here concern us. There is no doubt that Irenaeus was on the right track.

As a theologian, Irenaeus was still a man of his times. For him, God the Father was a simple being, without parts, without passions—in other words, the One of Later Platonism in Christian dress—and God the Son, the *Logos*, is his revelation. The Holy Spirit, however, is seen in a more positive light than was the case with Justin. It (and one really cannot refer to the Holy Spirit as he or she) is 'our communication with Christ, the pledge of incorruptibility, the strengthening of our faith, the ladder of ascent to God',[3] and as the Holy Spirit prepares us for the Son of God, so the Son leads us to the Father, and the Father bestows upon us incorruption and immortality. And again, reflecting the Platonic subordinationism in which each rung of the ladder is lower than that above it, Irenaeus tells us that we ascend to the Son through the Spirit, and to the Father through the Son. In other words, our redemption involves the whole Trinity just as creation involved the whole Trinity. The Son and the Holy Spirit are called the 'two hands of God', and in creating the worlds God has no need of any other helpers,assistants, angels, or gnostic *aeons*. His Word (*Logos*) and his Wisdom, the Son and the Spirit, were always with him, and 'through them and in them he made all things by his own free will'.[4]

---

[2]Irenaeus, *Adversus Haereses*, 3.3.1.

[3]*Ibid.*, 3.24.1.

[4]*Ibid.*,4.20.1. See also, *ibid.*5.1.2–3.

The theology of Irenaeus, then, is more distinctly trinitarian than that of Justin and represents the culmination of
Christian thought in the second century. His views on the
incarnation and the theology of 'recapitulation' we shall
leave aside until we deal with the great Christological
controversy, but for all its coherence, the theology of
Irenaeus leaves many questions unanswered. There is still
a long way to go before the nature, role, and relationship of
the three persons of the Trinity are clearly and unequivocally presented, and to pursue our investigations to the
next stage we must return from the west to the east, from
Gaul to Egypt, from Lyons to one of the greatest intellectual centres of the Roman world: Alexandria.

S<small>T</small> P<small>ETER</small>. Constantinople, sixth- or seventh-century.

THE PHILOSOPHER PLATO. Antique fourth-century (b.c.e.) marble copy, after a bronze original of Silanion.

CHAPTER IV

CHRISTIAN PLATONISM AND
THE SCHOOL OF ALEXANDRIA

WE SAW IN THE FIRST CHAPTER how Christianity, despite persecution, still managed to attract converts, and it seems that among these early converts many were women and slaves. Indeed, Christianity seems to have been particularly attractive to women, for it could offer a system in which both sexes were equal before God (if not before the members of the Christian community), in which marriage was regarded as a serious and binding contract, not to be undertaken lightly, and in which sexual sins committed by a husband were, at least in theory, as serious as those committed by a wife. But in Roman society women and slaves were not, on the whole, well educated, and although the pagan opponents of Christianity overstressed the point, the Christian communities of the first two centuries were not noted for their intellectual acumen.

In the early years of the third century, however, this unfortunate situation began to change as more and more converts from the better-educated classes made their way into Christianity. These converts then demanded of their new faith a system of thought which would be as intellec-

tually satisfying and as comprehensively presented as any
of the other systems of the day (including Gnosticism), and
they were certainly not satisfied with the undemanding
pastoral writings of the Apostolic Fathers or the apologetic-
oriented theology of Justin and his associates.

To respond to this demand and to provide what was
needful there came into being the Catechetical School
of Alexandria. Its first known teacher was Pantaenus (he
probably came from Sicily, and was a convert from Stoicism), but it reached its greatest heights under the
successors of Pantaenus: Clement of Alexandria and the
brilliant and original Origen. The characteristics of Alexandrian teaching were threefold, and each of the three
points follows logically from that which precedes it. First of
all, in the School of Alexandria we see the most comprehensive adaptation of Later Platonism to Christianity ever
to be attempted in the Christian tradition, either before or
(with very few exceptions) since. Secondly, just as Platonism laid great stress on the spiritual side of things (it was,
as we noted earlier, an *idealistic*, not a materialistic, philosophy), so, too, the Christian Platonists of Alexandria were
far happier when dealing with the spiritual world than
with the material one. Thus, as we shall see later, they
tended to stress the divinity of Christ at the expense of his
humanity, and, as happened in the case of Origen, their
insistence on the utter transcendence and purity of God
the Father/the Platonic One could lead to grossly exaggerated subordinationism. Thirdly, their approach to scripture and its exegesis mirrored this otherworldly concern.
They looked for the hidden and spiritual meaning of the
text—the mystical meaning—rather than the literal and
historical meaning, and their allegorical interpretations
could lead them into rarefied heights of ethereal exegesis
which are sometimes wholly splendid and sometimes
plainly bizarre.

All three of these factors may be seen at work in Clement and Origen, and we may therefore turn our attention to the first of these theologians, who, born of pagan parents, probably in Athens, came to Alexandria after extensive travels and succeeded Pantaenus as head of the catechetical school sometime in the last decade of the second century.

Clement shared many of Justin's concerns, and the difference between them is a difference of degree rather than of kind. Clement still finds it necessary to defend the Christian tradition against both pagans and Gnostics, but whereas his attitude to the former is predictable (we find him opposing the superstition and immorality of many of the pagan cults with the reasonableness and moral virtue of Christianity), his approach to the latter is more interesting. He does not attack the Gnostics in the same way as Irenaeus of Lyons, but rather takes over their essential principles and reapplies them to Christianity. What is the Gnostic claim? That they possess knowledge. Just so, says Clement, but Christianity possesses the *true* knowledge, the full knowledge of God revealed by the *Logos*, the revelation of God, and found in Scripture and the Christian tradition. But surely the Gnostics, too, maintain that they have a secret tradition? Just so, says Clement, but the tradition of Christianity is more authoritative and more venerable: it was entrusted to the Apostles by the Son of God himself, and from them has been transmitted from father to son down to the church of his own times. This is the 'renowned and august Rule of the Tradition'[1] which Christianity alone possesses, and which comprises the true knowledge, the true *gnōsis*. Are we then saying that Christians are actually Gnostics? Just so, says Clement, but there are two sorts of Gnostic: the false Gnostic, who belongs to one of the many Gnostic sects, and the True Gnostic, who

---

[1]Clement, *Stromateis* 1.1.

is the Christian. Christianity, therefore, is the True Gnosticism, and if it was possible for the false Gnosticism to use pagan philosophy to present a comprehensive and intellectually stimulating system, the True Gnosticism—on the principle that anything you can do we can do better—can do so as well.

Clement is in full agreement with Justin that God the *Logos*, the second person of the Trinity, is the source of all true inspiration, but he goes further than Justin in his willingness to see in philosophy a true preparation for the gospel. Until the incarnation, he says, philosophy was essential to the Greeks for righteousness, but even after the incarnation it may still prove useful in leading them to Christ. What the Law of Moses was for the Jews, philosophy was for the Greeks. Both are 'schoolteachers' or 'pedagogues' (Clement borrows the term—*paidagōgos* in Greek—from Galatians 3:24) leading their pupils directly to Christianity.

Clement, therefore, and the whole of the Alexandrian School, have no hesitation at all in using Platonism and Stoicism to explain and interpret the Christian tradition. He actually refers to God the Father as the One, adding that he is beyond form, beyond limit, beyond conception, beyond description. In his writings there are many passages where it would be very difficult (unless one knew the author) to decide if one were reading the work of a Christian or a hard-line Platonist. The Son he refers to as Mind—the Divine Mind of Later Platonism—and this Mind became man in order to provide the human race with the most complete and perfect revelation possible, and enable humankind to progress slowly but steadily in the knowledge of God. Nor does this progress end with death. After we have passed from this world, our sins are purged by fire (but Clement is thinking more of the 'rational gaseous fire' of the Stoics than the straightforward flames of the Christian hell), and we progress from mansion to mansion (and in my Father's house, said Jesus of Nazareth, there are many mansions [Jn 14:2]) to such heights and such bliss as we cannot in this world conceive.

Later generations found some of Clement's views unacceptable. As a Christian Gnostic he tended to lay too much stress on knowledge at the expense of faith, and his emphasis on knowledge led him to see ignorance as a greater evil than sin. His Platonism led him, inevitably, into subordinationism, and his Stoicism produced some very curious views about the humanity of Christ. In his successor, Origen, we see even more peculiarities, and despite (or because of) the brilliance and originality of many of his theories, there was scarcely one which was not the subject of later ecclesiastical condemnation, and scarcely any which made their way unchanged into the body of the Christian tradition.

Clement was forced to flee Alexandria in about 202 as a consequence of persecution (he died, still far from Egypt, shortly before 215), and his place as head of the Catechetical School was taken by the formidable Origen. At this time he was probably no more than twenty—a brilliant, fervent, enthusiastic, and deeply committed youth—and following his appointment, he began to lead a life of strict asceticism and discipline. It was probably about this time that he interpreted Matthew 19:12 in rather too literal a way, and castrated himself. He travelled widely in subsequent years and was eventually ordained priest in Palestine in the year 230. Demetrius, bishop of Alexandria, objected to this (he considered the ordination to have been irregular) and deprived Origen both of his position as head of the Catechetical School and of his priesthood. He then exiled him to Caesarea where he established another school which soon achieved great fame, and continued his literary activities unabated for a further twenty years. In 250 he was caught up in the persecution of the emperor Decius, imprisoned, and tortured. He died at Tyre, his health broken as a result of his sufferings, in about 254. He was just about seventy years old.

It is easy, as well as tempting, to spend too long on Origen. There is no doubt that he was one of the greatest and most original thinkers in the whole history of early Christianity—certainly the greatest and most original in the period before the Council of Nicaea—but fascinating though his views may be, there is little point in spending a great deal of time in explaining ideas which, for a Christian, were decidedly idiosyncratic and which, for the most part, the later church wholeheartedly condemned. We shall not linger, therefore, over his doctrine of the pre-existence of souls, or his theory of how these souls fell, or his explanation of how one of them was to become the soul of Christ, or his view that at the end of all things, all creatures, including Satan, will be redeemed and saved. His main importance for us lies in his attitude to the biblical text and its interpretation, and in one or two comments on the nature of the Trinity which anticipate the great Trinitarian controversy of the fourth century.

Before we begin, however, a word of caution is necessary: because Origen's works were vehemently condemned and because their inordinate length made them difficult to copy, many of his writings have perished, and what survives survives, for the most part, either in fragments or in Latin translation. This introduces two problems: firstly, because of the nature of the fragments it is not always clear whether Origen is setting forth a thesis to be accepted or a suggestion to be discussed; secondly, one of his translators, Rufinus of Aquileia (c. 345–410), admired Origen tremendously and was quite prepared to 'amend' a text if he thought that by so doing he could bring it more in line with prevailing orthodox opinion. Our approach to Origen, therefore, must be tempered with caution, for there is always a danger in postulating a particular type of forest from the existence of a few stunted trees.

Origen, like Clement, still found it necessary to defend Christianity (the Edicts of Toleration were still about a century away), and in his disputations with the Jews of the empire, he realized that if one were going to argue from the text of scripture, one needed a reliable text to argue from. Both the Christian churches and the Greek synagogues of his day used a Greek translation of the Old Testament (the New Testament, of course, had been written in Greek from the start), but the four major versions in circulation had considerable divergences among them. Origen therefore produced a colossal compilation of these versions, and included with them the original Hebrew text together with its transliteration in Greek characters. And since the whole work was arranged in six columns—the Hebrew text, its transliteration, and the four Greek translations—it became known as the *Hexapla*, a word which means 'six-fold' in Greek. The entire work was so huge that it may never have been copied in its entirety (it survives only in fragments), but it is the earliest example we have of a Christian attempt at providing a basis for scientific textual criticism.

In his attitude to the biblical text, Origen exemplifies the allegorical character of the entire School of Alexandria. Not only did this reflect the idealistic approach of Platonism, but it was also directly opposed to the views of certain semi-Christian Gnostics (Marcion in particular) who held that Scripture could be understood only in a literal sense. Origen disagreed profoundly with this, convinced that behind the most mundane and seemingly uninspired passages of the Old and New Testaments spiritual truths could be discerned. The literal meaning is important, Origen had no doubt of that, but it is much less important than the allegorical meaning; and a passage in, say, Joshua may tell us not only of conditions in Canaan many centuries ago (this is the 'body' of the text), but also indicate something of the ideal structure of the Christian church (this is the 'soul' of the text), or even (at the highest level, which is the 'spirit' of the text) inform us of the nature of the relationship between the individual soul and God. Origen's so-called 'mysticism'—his delineation of the long and arduous path which leads eventually to the mystical union, or mystical marriage, between the soul and the *Logos*—is simply a reflection and a corollary of this allegorical tendency. His soul, like the Platonic bird in its cage (an analogy we used in Chapter II), was continually flapping its wings against the door. Given the slightest chance, the tiniest chink, it was out and off, rising from the literal world to the giddy heights of the spiritual heavens, so that by beginning with an Old Testament discussion of the Israelite law of inheritance from Numbers 27, Origen can end with the face-to-face vision of God, when we, too, shall become gods in Jesus Christ. This mode of exegesis had a profound and lasting effect upon the Christian tradition, and although it reached its apogee with the writers of the Middle Ages, it may still be witnessed in operation, with more or (usually) less success, in the Christian pulpits of our present day.

Biblical interpretation was Origen's prime concern, and his indefatigable energy produced multitudinous commentaries of inordinate length. Yet he did not confine his talents to pure exegesis but turned them also to the preparation of the first comprehensive and systematic textbook of Christian theology. This was what the better educated and more cultured Christian converts demanded, and this was what Christianity had never had. The work was entitled *On First Principles* and was divided into four books: the first book dealt with celestial matters (Father, Son, and Holy Spirit, together with angels and other heavenly things); the second with earthly concerns (the world and its creation, the human race, the soul, the incarnation, and so on); the third with psychological questions (free will and its consequences); and the fourth with scripture, its inspiration and interpretation. Despite the fact that it contained numerous ideas which the church later condemned, the volume was a remarkable achievement and provides a fascinating glimpse into the thought-world of third-century Christian Platonism.

It is curious, however, that although Origen utilizes Platonism to an even greater extent than Clement, he also maintains that one should treat it with the utmost care. He never says, as Clement said, that philosophy is a guide to Christ, and his attitude to the philosophers, including Plato, was overtly critical. Yet none was more deeply influenced by the ideas and outlook of Platonism, and Origen, in this matter, exemplifies the dictum 'Do as I say, not as I do'. His Platonism is clearly evident in his doctrine of the Trinity, for just as he is the most Platonic of third-century Christians, so, too, he is one of the most subordinationist. God the Father, as we would expect, is the One of Later Platonism, but although the Son/*Logos* is his true revelation, he is decidedly subordinate to the Father. Origen calls him a 'second god' and says, without hesitation, that the Son and the Holy Spirit excel all created things to a degree which precludes comparison since it is beyond all measure, but that they are themselves excelled by the Father 'by just as much or even more'.[2]

If the Father is Goodness, the Son is the image of that Goodness; if the Father is True God, the Son is merely God; and although the Son shares with the Father an identity of will, Origen quoted with approval that statement from the gospel of John which was to prove so embarrassing for those who later opposed subordinationism: 'The Father is greater than I (Jn 14:28). As to the Holy Spirit, Origen appears undecided as to whether he should place it with the Creator (as the third and lowest principle of the Godhead), or with the creation (as the highest of all created things), and he is somewhat reticent about admitting its divinity. Yet for all this subordinationism, Origen introduces into his doctrine of the Trinity two concepts which were to be of first importance in events occurring a century later: the first being the idea of eternal generation, and the second, the term *homoousios*.

---

[2]Origen, *Commentary on John* 13. 25.

Eternal generation means that when the Father put forth or produced or generated the Son, he did not do so in the same way as a woman brings forth a baby, or a bullet comes out of a gun. In both these cases, the action is a *single* action, done once and for all. But when a candle shines and gives forth its light, the light is emitted continually so long as the flame is burning. It is a *continual* act, not a single action, and it is in this way that God the Son is begotten. God the Father continually pours forth God the Son, just as the rational human mind continually generates human will (this is Origen's own analogy), and since God the Father is eternal and has never been without the Son (for Origen learned from St John that 'he was with God in the beginning' [Jn 1:2]), so it follows that in the case of God, continual generation is *eternal* generation. From the beginning of eternity to its end, God the Father generates the Son as light forever generates its own radiance (again, the analogy is Origen's own). Light without radiance is unthinkable, says Origen, and more than that, light and its radiance show a community of substance. In other words we have here *light* from light (the analogy is an old Platonic one), not trees from light or heat from light or horses from light; but as a river puts forth a stream (water from water) or the rational mind puts forth its will (mind from mind), what is put forth here is the same 'stuff' or 'material' or 'substance' as that which puts it forth. Father and Son, light and splendour, river and stream, mind and will are each *consubstantial*, 'of the same substance', and since the Greek word for 'same' is *homos* and the Greek word for 'substance' is *ousia*, the two terms combine to form the adjective *homo-ousios*.

For the moment we will say no more about this important term, and whether Origen himself elaborated on it is something we do not know. Most of his writings, as we have mentioned, have come down to us only in fragments, and it is only in a fragment that this term *homoousios* is found. Indeed, it is not even certain that the word is

Origen's own. Despite its appearance in a portion of his authentic writings, it might have been added by Rufinus, who, in ceaselessly looking after Origen's interests, may have inserted the term at a later date to improve his master's image. But whether Origen himself used it or not, there is no doubt that its prominence in the third century could not compare with its importance in the fourth, when it was introduced into the Creed of Nicaea and championed by the great Athanasius (against strong opposition) as the very watchword of orthodoxy. To this development we must now turn, for the death of Origen occurred at much the same time as the birth of Arius, who was destined to become the first of the great heresiarchs and shake the Christian church to its very foundations.

THE COUNCIL OF CONSTANTINOPLE. Adapted from a ninth-century depictation showing the Emperor Theodorius, patriachs, and priests gathered in Council. The open Scripture on the throne symbolizes the presence of Christ, the Word of God.

CHAPTER V

ARIUS AND
THE COUNCIL OF NICAEA

THE EDICTS OF TOLERATION enacted between 311 and 313 (whatever they might have been) had a profound effect on Christianity, as we saw in the first chapter. With external persecution removed, the mind of the church became occupied not with survival, but with theology, and the topic which concerned it more than any other was the relationship of Father and Son in the doctrine of the Trinity. Because of the deep influence of later Platonism, Christian writers up to the early fourth century had all been subordinationists, but because theological thought, like all other thought, develops and progresses, ideas once acceptable were no longer found to be so.

These developments came to a head in the first quarter of the fourth century when the priest in charge of one of the most important churches in Alexandria began to teach publicly that not only was Christ subordinate to the Father, but that 'there was, when he was not'. The priest was Arius, a man who had been trained in Antioch in Syria, not Alexandria, and who was noted for the excellence of his preaching and the purity of his life. But what did he mean by 'there was, when he was not'? Stated rather more crudely than ever Arius did, he meant that there was a time (a term Arius himself avoids since all this happened before time began) when Christ the Son did not exist as a separate and distinct person of the Trinity. In the beginning there was only God the Father, who contained within himself the *potential* for the Son (we see here the clear influence of Platonic thought) and then, sometime 'later' brought the Son into being as the second person of the Trinity. There was therefore a 'time' when the second person of the Trinity had no separate reality but existed only in poten-tiality in the mind of the Father. But even after he was brought forth, this second person of the Trinity was subor-dinate to the first: because he came into being by an act of the Father's will, he could be called a 'creature' or 'a created thing' ('but not,' says Arius, very cautiously, 'as one of the creatures'), and as a 'creature' or 'a created thing', he was not of the same substance (*ousia*) as the Father. And since he was not of the same substance (*ousia*) as the Father, he was not really and truly God. He was God by *grace*, not by *nature*; he was God because God the Father graciously permitted him to be God and bestowed upon him certain attributes of divinity, but he was not God in his own right, in his own being, in his own *substance*.

It is impossible for us here to do full justice to the thought of Arius. His ideas actually had considerable subtlety, and he seems to have taken great care in the way he expressed them. It is even possible that in one particular area he was deliberately misrepresented by his opponents: according to them, Arius not only stated that the Son was a 'creature' or 'created thing', but that like all other creatures, includ-ing the world and us in it, he had been created by God the Father out of nothing. This would indeed be an outrageous statement, but a very persuasive case has been argued that he never did say it. It may well have been put in his mouth by his rivals to make him appear worse than he was. His later followers maintained it, that is true, but disciples are frequently more extreme than their master. On the other hand, what a person says is often less important than what other people think he says, and however much we try to defend Arius, there is not the least doubt that he was subordinationist, and that as far as he was concerned, he was simply teaching what had been taught by two successive centuries of Christian theologians. For our purposes, therefore, we may summarize the essential points of his teaching as follows: (1) there was a 'time' when God the Son did not exist as a separate and distinct person of the Trinity; (2) God the Son is subordinate to God the Father; (3) God the Son is not truly God by nature; and (4) God the Son is not of the same substance as God the Father.

The next question we must ask is why these ideas were thought to be incorrect. If this sort of thinking had developed without question for a couple of hundred years, why did it suddenly seem wrong? It is clear from the writings of Arius' opponents, particularly Athanasius the Great, that there were three things wrong with it, and these three things are as relevant for Christianity today as they were for Christianity in the fourth century. Arian subordinationism does not work, and the reasons why it does not work are as follows: firstly, Christianity has always maintained that God is, in some way, One *and Three*. This is one of the main features which distinguishes Christianity from the other great monotheistic systems, Judaism and Islam, both of which assert that God is One Alone. God *is* One and Three, say the Christians, he always *was* One and Three, and always *will be* One and Three. Did Arius say this? No, he did not. According to his teaching, at the beginning of all things there was only God the Father, One Alone, and then, sometime 'later' (though Arius never uses so crude a word), there came into being God the Son, and 'later' still, the Holy Spirit. So, according to Arius, there was a time when God was *not* One and Three, and whatever that is (says Athanasius), it is not Christianity.

Secondly, Christianity has always maintained that worship may be offered only to God. To worship anything less than God—angels or pagan deities or kings or emperors or animals or anything else—is idolatry, the worship of idols. Indeed, it was for this principle (as we saw in Chapter I) that so many Christian martyrs had died in so many appalling ways. But if, as Arius maintained, God the Son was subordinate to God the Father and was not truly God, then to worship Christ was to worship a being less than God, and to worship a being less than God (said Athanasius again) is not Christianity, but idolatry.

Thirdly, Christianity maintains that salvation involves two essential principles: (1) that the iniquities of the human race have been forgiven and its many sins paid for by the death of Christ on Calvary, and (2) that this same human race is, by God's grace, permitted to share in the divine nature of Christ and become, in a sense, divine. The New Testament says this (2 Peter 1:3–4) and the early church Fathers had no doubt that this was true. But to redeem the whole of the human race, past, present, and future, from all its infinite wickedness requires an infinite being, and the only infinite being is God. And as for the second point, we may summarize the principle in a phrase much loved by the Greek writers: 'God became human that in him humans might become god'. They did not mean by this that 'a 70% God became human that humans might become 70% god'. In other words, if Christ was not *fully* God, not *truly* God, not *100%* God, then (1) redemption might not be complete (for perhaps a 70% God could only redeem 70% of humanity from 70% of its sins), and (2) the New Testament is wrong, and we are not going to share in the full divine nature, but only in a semi-divine nature, a 60% or 70% divine nature, a second best. And that, said Athanasius for a third time, is not Christianity.

Arius, therefore, was teaching a doctrine which, although it had a long and uncontested history, was actually unchristian and idolatrous, and when Alexander, his bishop, heard about it, probably sometime in 318, he ordered him to cease. Arius refused. Why should he? This was what Origen had taught; this was what everyone had taught; this was the tradition. Alexander summoned a synod of Egyptian bishops to consider the matter, and as a result of their deliberations, Arius' teaching was condemned. To this he strongly objected and immediately sought support for himself and his doctrines among his friends at Antioch, where, it will be remembered, he had been trained. Some of those he contacted were exceedingly powerful, and one in particular, Eusebius, the bishop of Nicomedia, was a great friend of the imperial family and had far-reaching influence at court. It was he who would baptize Constantine on his deathbed, and there is no doubt that the emperor listened attentively to his ideas and suggestions. Furthermore, between Antioch and Alexandria there existed considerable rivalry, both political and theological, for both had Catechetical Schools and differed markedly in their outlook. Arius' appeal to his fellow Antiochenes, and the intervention of the powerful Eusebius, transformed what began as a local theological dispute into a political-geographical-theological power struggle which split the Christian world in two.

Constantine, of course, was horrified, and after consulting his ecclesiastical adviser, a westerner named Hosius (or Ossius), who was bishop of Cordoba in Spain, decided to send him to Alexandria to see if he could resolve the issue. Hosius, predictably, did not succeed. The conflict by now was far too intense, far too political, and far too violent for any such intervention to have any effect, and the situation was not helped by the fact that Hosius himself was strongly partisan and heavily biased against Arius. Constantine therefore summoned a Council of bishops, the first ecumenical Council. His original intention was that it should meet at Ancyra (now the city of Ankara, the capital of modern Turkey) in 325. But after witnessing the underhanded operations of Hosius, who, in a number of ways, had attempted to prejudge the issue, Constantine relocated the Council and commanded that it meet at Nicaea (the modern Iznik in northwest Turkey), which was conveniently situated near the imperial residence from which the Emperor himself could keep on eye on things.

Thus it was that the great Council of Nicaea convened in the early summer of 325 to consider, and ultimately to condemn, the teachings of Arius. We do not know precisely how many bishops attended. The traditional number is 318, but this number was almost certainly stolen from the book of Genesis (Genesis 14:14: the number of Abram's servants), and the actual total was probably fewer. Almost all who attended were from the Greek-speaking east. The representatives of the west were Hosius of Cordoba, two priests who represented the Pope of the time (Silvester I, whose involvement in the great controversy was wholly insignificant), and five other bishops. Constantine himself opened the proceedings and kept a careful watch on them throughout, but his interest was not theological (he was not too concerned as to which side won, and his understanding of the theological points at issue left much to be desired), but political. What Constantine demanded was a resolution of the conflict and an end to the theological civil war which was threatening his empire.

If ever there were *acta* or minutes of the Council, these have been lost; all that survives is the letters calling the Council together, twenty miscellaneous canons or decrees dealing with a variety of subjects (e.g., the order of rank of the great metropolitan sees; certain other heresies apart from that of Arius; how one should deal with those who lapsed in recent persecutions; how one should pray during the paschal season), and the very important Creed of Nicaea, of which the following is a literal translation:

> We believe in one God, Father, almighty, maker of all things, visible and invisible; and in one Lord Jesus Christ, the Son of God, begotten from the Father, only-begotten, that is, from the substance (*ousia*) of

the Father, God from God, light from light, true God from true God, begotten not made, consubstantial (*homoousios*) with the Father, through whom all things came into being, both things in heaven and things on earth; who, because of us humans and because of our salvation, came down and became incarnate, and became human; he suffered and rose on the third day, he ascended into the heavens, and he will come to judge the living and the death; and in the Holy Spirit.

But as for those who say, 'There was, when he was not', and 'Before he was begotten, he was not', and that 'he came into existence out of nothing',. or who allege the Son of God to be 'Of a different *hypostasis* or substance (*ousia*)' or 'created', or 'changeable', or 'mutable': these the holy universal and apostolic church anathematizes.

This creed, which was drawn up only after considerable discussion, was signed by all but two of the bishops at the Council. The two errant members were immediately deposed and sent home. But it is not so much a statement of what the orthodox Christians believed as what the Arians believed and, as a consequence, what the orthodox would not accept. Look at the language: (1) the Son is *begotten* from the Father, and not, as the Arians say, created or made; (2) the Son is *true God*, and not, as the Arians say, something subordinate; and (3) the Son is of the same substance as the Father, *consubstantial* with the Father, and not, as the Arians say, of a different substance or *ousia*. He is God from God and light from light (here is the old Platonic analogy reappearing), and not 'partly God from fully God' or 'dullness from brilliance'. And in the use of the term consubstantial/*homoousios* (a word, it will be remembered, which Origen may have used), the Nicene Fathers intended to imply the utter impossibility of subordinationism. How? Let us consider the question.

Firstly, what is God the Father made of? What is his substance or *ousia*? *Answer*: his substance is 'divinity' or 'deity' or 'god-ness'. Secondly, if we dig a channel from one huge lake to lead into and form another huge lake, is there any difference between the water in the two lakes? *Answer*: no, there is no difference. The chemical composition is the same; the wetness is the same; the colour is the same; the substance or *ousia* is the same. The water in the second lake is not 'weaker' than that in the first; nor is it less thirst-quenching; nor is there less of it. In other words, if two realities share the same substance—if they are *homoousios*—their properties are identical. Thirdly, how does this apply to the Father and the Son? *Answer*: if the Father's substance is pure 'god-ness' and the substance of the Son is the same as that of the Father, then the substance of the Son is also pure 'god-ness'. And just as water is water is water, or light is light is light, or a rose is a rose is a rose, so true godness is godness is godness, and the consubstantial Son cannot be any less than, weaker than, inferior to, or subordinate to, the consubstantial Father. Two realities which share the same substance share the same powers and the same properties, and that is all there is to it. Arius and the Arians are totally wrong, and subordinationism is wholly incompatible with orthodox Christian belief.

It was these ideas which the Fathers at Nicaea (or to be more accurate, some of the Fathers at Nicaea) wished to imply by the use of the term *homoousios*. But before considering the consequences of their decision, let us take note of two other points in the Creed they drew up. First of all, notice the brevity of the clause referring to the Holy Spirit. We believe, they said, 'in the Holy Spirit as well', and that is all they said. To learn about the Holy Spirit as lord and lifegiver, who spoke through the prophets, and so on, we must wait some fifty years. The dispute at Nicaea was a dispute about two persons of the Trinity, not about three, and the question of the nature of the Holy Spirit still awaited discussion. In any case, as we remarked earlier, the Creed of Nicaea was not intended to be a comprehensive summary of orthodox Christian belief. We should see it more as a particular response to an emergency situation, and it answers the specific question 'Are you orthodox in what you believe of the Son of God?' It does not answer the general question 'What should an orthodox Christian believe?'

Secondly, notice the anathemas which appear at the end of the Creed. These present a neat summary of Arian doctrine, and they were originally an integral part of the text. But with the final defeat of Arianism in the later fourth century, they began to lose their importance, and later creeds rarely included them. Only one church—the Armenian Orthodox Church—still retains them as part of the liturgy to the present day.

We have seen in this chapter how the views of Arius were wrong. However subtly they were presented, they contained ideas which, by the early fourth century, were recognized as being incompatible with the Christian tradition. We have seen, too, how a theological dispute was transformed into a political and geographical conflict, and how the Council of Nicaea was called in an attempt to resolve the situation. And we have seen, finally, how the bishops at the council drew up a statement of orthodox opinion on the question of the divinity of the Son, and how the term *homoousios* was intended to imply the identity of substance of Father and Son, and hence the impossibility that the one could be inferior to the other. Unfortunately, this was not the only thing that the word *homoousios* could imply, and far from resolving the Arian dispute, it only exacerbated the situation and, as we shall see in our next chapter, led to problems of even greater complexity.

ARIANS FLEEING. Adapted from a ninth-century illumination.

CHAPTER VI

THE TRIUMPH OF
THE NICENE FAITH

ID THE COUNCIL OF NICAEA resolve the Arian question? Of course not. People do not change their minds simply because they are told to do so, and a signature is a cheap enough way to escape the ire of an emperor. It is true that all but two of the bishops signed the Creed and thus, in theory, agreed to the condemnation of Arius and the use of the term *homoousios*, but it is also true that many of them—perhaps the majority—were uncomfortable with the term and not all of them understood it in the same way. And some of them, of course, were just plain playing it safe under the watchful eye of Constantine.

But why were so many opposed to its use? Three reasons stand out. First, because the word was not biblical. It was certainly used by the Later Platonists, but it does not occur either in the New Testament or in the Greek translation of the Old Testament. Was it wise, then, to place so much importance on a term which had no scriptural—and therefore no divine—authority? Secondly, the word had been used previously, but by people whose opinions were highly suspect. Some of the Gnostic sects had used it, and it had also been associated with the doctrines of a certain

Paul of Samosata, who had been consecrated bishop of Antioch in about 260 and condemned and deposed in 268. Paul was more Jewish than Christian and held views even more extreme than those of Arius. For him, God the Father and God the Son never became truly separate and distinct, and he saw Jesus of Nazareth as no more than a uniquely inspired man. Paul, in fact, was unitarian, not trinitarian, and the church was perfectly justified in condemning his views. Thirdly —and this is the most important point—the word really was ambiguous. It could mean what it was intended to mean: that Father and Son *shared* the same substance; but it could also mean something quite different: that Father and Son *were* the same substance or, in other words, the same person. And there is a wealth of difference between saying that Adolf Hitler and Winston Churchill shared a common substance (i.e., 'human-ness') and that Hitler and Churchill were secretly the same man. It was in this second sense (*homoousios* = 'same *person*') that the notorious Paul of Samosata had used the word, and it was for primarily this reason that a large number of the Nicene Fathers disliked and distrusted it.

Some of them, therefore, suggested a compromise. Why not avoid the dangerous word 'same' (*homos*) and say instead that Father and Son are of *similar* substance? If two things are similar, they cannot possibly be one and the same. Similarity demands duality: you cannot be similar to yourself. Furthermore, said these compromisers and Middle-of-the-Roaders, the change in terminology is a tiny one. In Greek the word for 'same' is *homos* and the word for 'similar' is *homoios*, and if we conjoin these terms with the word for 'substance,' *ousia*, then there is only a difference of a single letter: *homo-ousios* = 'of the same substance' and *homoi-ousios* = 'of similar substance.'

This suggestion fell on welcome ears, and many embraced it eagerly. It could so easily mean whatever you wanted it to mean. Those who were more orthodox could interpret it as meaning 'The substance of Father and Son is similar [in every possible way, and the Son is the very image of the Father]'; and those who were still, at heart, more Arian (but who were not going to admit it) could interpret it as meaning 'The substance of Father and Son is similar [in a few minor ways, and we still think that the Son is an inferior being].' In other words, the great advantage and great disadvantage of the word was its breadth of meaning: we know what colour black is, and we know what colour white is, but there are a thousand shades of grey.

What this meant, then, was that whereas before Nicaea there were two main parties, Arian and anti-Arian, after Nicaea there were three. The situation can be likened to a human body: to the head correspond those who were fully orthodox, who understood what the term *homoousios* was supposed to mean and who were willing and eager to use it; to the feet correspond the hard-line Arians who never did accept the term and who, like Arius himself, still thought that Father and Son were of *different* substance; and to the mass in the middle, from shoulders to shins, correspond those who preferred *homoiousios*—of *similar* substance—and amongst this very large company there were all shades of opinion as to just how similar the similarity was.

It is at this point that we must introduce Athanasius the Great. Born in Alexandria in about 295, he was trained in the Catechetical School of his native city, made a deacon in 319, and, as secretary, attended Alexander, the bishop of Alexandria, at the Council of Nicaea in 325. On Alexander's death in 328, he succeeded him as bishop and ,still in his early thirties, became the greatest and most outspoken defender of Nicene orthodoxy and the term *homoousios*. As a consequence he also became the greatest and most hated enemy of the Arians. The task of Athanasius was two-fold: first to oppose, and then to reconcile. For some twenty years, from about 340 to 360, he opposed the Arians in every possible way. He produced a series of treatises to demonstrate where they were wrong and why they were wrong, and to set forth as clearly as possible the faith declared at Nicaea: God the Son was truly God and had never been anything less. And then, from about 360 onwards, he turned his attention to that large party of Middle-of-the-Roaders who were, on the whole, orthodox in their opinions (they acknowledged that Christ was fully God), but who preferred to use the term *homoiousios* rather than the dangerous *homoousios*. These he strove to reconcile and bring into the Nicene fold. He had to prove to them that *homoiousios* was even more dangerous than *homoousios* (which indeed it was: there are far too many shades of similarity) and persuade them that *homoousios*, or consubstantial, was the only safe, accurate, and precise term to use—the only term which left no doubt at all about the full divinity of Father and Son, and the only term which excluded Arianism totally and completely. The extent to which he succeeded in both these endeavours is Athanasius' outstanding achievement.

His efforts, however, were not helped by circumstances, for the problems which arose after Nicaea were not only theological, but political. Indeed, there was little in the early church in which politics did not play a part, and the inspiration of the Holy Spirit was all too often mediated by blackmail, bribery, and intimidation. So long as Constantine was alive, the Nicene Creed remained the standard of orthodoxy, but even during that time the Arian party worked hard to recoup its losses. Its most formidable ally was Eusebius, the bishop of Nicomedia, whom we met earlier, who still had the ear of Constantine and who, with great skill and considerable success, continually attempted to undermine the efforts of Athanasius. But after the death of Constantine in 337 the situation became utterly chaotic. Successive rulers were either pro-Arian, anti-Arian, or tolerant of both, and who was bishop in what diocese and at what time depended almost entirely on the theological viewpoint of the emperor or his advisers. Prelates moved in and out of their sees with astonishing speed, and Athanasius himself was exiled and restored to Alexandria no less than five times, spending some seventeen years in exile. This chaotic state of affairs came to an end only in 381, two years after Theodosius I had become emperor. After first outlawing paganism (as we saw in Chapter I) and making Christianity the official state religion, he also decreed that Arianism should be considered a legal offence, and from the end of the fourth century it played no further significant role in the eastern Roman world. This is not to say that it was completely dead: it was a singularly hardy heresy, and after being extirpated from the centre of the empire, it took root among those who inhabited its extremities—primarily the Teutonic tribes—and flourished there for many more disreputable decades. That, however, is another story and need not concern us for the present.

Throughout these fifty or so years of political intrigue and party politics, Athanasius, whether in or out of exile, had been labouring assiduously on behalf of the faith of Nicaea. Again and again he had stressed the essential points: true redemption demands that Christ be true God; the Son is generated eternally from the substance of the Father; an eternal Father therefore implies an eternal Son; as the sun forever pours forth its radiance, so the light which is the Father forever pours forth the light which is the Son; but if, as Father and Son, they are two realities, yet as one God they are one substance; and if both share the same substance, both share the same power, the same glory, the same divinity, the same 'god-ness'; and how is this best expressed? Surely by the term *homoousios*, a word which demonstrates at one and the same time the divinity of Christ, the truth of Nicaea, and the error of the Arians.

By the time of Athanasius' death on 2 May 373, Arianism was on the decline. It would be another eight years before it was finally proscribed by Theodosius, but the intense efforts of Athanasius—and certain others, as we shall see in a moment—in the fifties and sixties of the fourth century had demonstrated clearly the theological inadequacies of Arianism and had succeeded in luring back into the Nicene fold a great many of the Middle-of-the-Roaders. One major problem still remained: if it were true that Father and Son were one God, yet two persons, and both fully divine, and if it were also true, as most now seemed prepared to accept, that the term *homoousios* best described their relationship, then what about the Holy Spirit? Was it, too, fully divine? Was it, too, *homoousios*? Was it, too, truly God?

The answer of Athanasius himself was quite clear and perfectly logical: (a) if God is really One as well as Three, then although there may be three persons, there can only be one nature or one substance; (b) if there is only one substance for one God, then obviously all three persons must share in it; therefore (c) the third person of the Trinity, like the second person of the Trinity, must also be consubstantial/*homoousios* with the Father; and (d) if the one God is truly eternal (and no Christian would deny it), then all three consubstantial persons must likewise be truly eternal, including the Holy Spirit. Furthermore, said Athanasius, if there is but one God and not three, then when God acts he must act as a unity. That is to say, since God is one, the Son or the Holy Spirit cannot act 'alone,' but always act in Trinity. How? Everything is effected *from* the Father *through* the Son *in* the Holy Spirit, and we may see this principle in operation in three examples. First of all, what happened at creation? Was it not God the Father who created the worlds? No: it was GOD THE FATHER through the Son in the Holy Spirit. But surely the Incarnation was the Incarnation of God the Son, not of God the Father? Yes: but the Incarnation was effected from the Father THROUGH THE SON in the Holy Spirit. We must not forget that although there is but one God, there are three distinct persons. And at Pentecost? Who descended in tongues of fire upon the astonished disciples? God the Holy Spirit, in a dramatic action which was accomplished from the Father through the Son IN THE HOLY SPIRIT. In other words, God the Trinity is one and indivisible (the words are those of Athanasius), and although there are three distinct persons, there is but 'one operation' and 'one activity.'

The teaching of Athanasius, therefore, is that the Trinity was (i) consubstantial; (ii) co-eternal; (iii) co-eternally distinct in its three persons; and (iv) of such a nature that when it acted, it acted as a unity. And this, essentially, is also the teaching of present-day Christianity.

Athanasius, however, was in advance of his time. *His* view of the Holy Spirit, and therefore of the Trinity, was what modern Christianity accepts, but it was not the view of many of his fellow priests and prelates. In 362, at a council held in Alexandria, Athanasius had managed to have accepted the proposition that the Holy Spirit was not a creature or something created, but was inseparable from the substance of Father and Son, yet by his death in 373 there was still no agreement on the matter and the question remained unresolved. Obviously something had to be done, and something was done by three remarkable theologians who flourished in the second half of the fourth century: Basil the Great (c. 330–379), bishop of Caesarea, a learned and holy man with a great talent for organization; his younger brother Gregory (c. 335 – c. 395), bishop of Nyssa, a man intimately acquainted with Later Platonic thought and possibly the most brilliant thinker of the period between Nicaea and Chalcedon; and their friend Gregory the Theologian (329–389), a learned and distinguished preacher, who was bishop of Sasima (a place he loathed) and assistant bishop to his father (also named Gregory), who held the see of Nazianzus. Since all three lived and worked in that part of modern Turkey which was once called Cappadocia, they are known collectively as the Cappadocian Fathers.

In one of the sermons of Gregory of Nazianzus we have a splendid example of the conflicting opinions about the nature of the Holy Spirit: some people, says Gregory, think it is an 'activity' or an 'energy'; some think it is a

'creature' or 'something created'; some, it is true, think
that it is 'God'; and some just don't know what to think.
And even of those who do acknowledge its divinity, some
are prepared to admit it openly, and some will only think
it, finding it wiser to keep their mouths shut. What the
Cappadocians did was put an end to this confusion and
complete the work of Athanasius. The latter had succeeded
in persuading most people to accept that Father and Son
were *homoousios*; he himself believed the same was true of
the Spirit; the Cappadocians had the responsibility of getting this view generally accepted.

It was no easy task: their main opponents were the
Pneumatomachians, a Greek word which means 'Those
who fight against the Spirit,' who pointed out that nowhere in Scripture is the Holy Spirit called 'God,' and that
in the places where it is mentioned, the clear implication is
that it is an inferior being. Nor could they conceive of any
relationship within the Trinity other than that of Father
and Son—a begetter and that which is begotten—and if we
are to start thinking of the Holy Spirit as the grandson of
the Father, then theology has become farcical. Against
these objections, the Cappadocians moved with deter-
mination combined with caution. Basil, the oldest of them,
began just by denying that the Spirit is a 'creature'; he then
moved on to say that it is inseparable from Father and Son,
and one with the divine nature; and finally (in 375) he
asserted that the Spirit must be numbered *with*, not *below*,
the Father and the Son and is to be accorded the same
glory, honour, and worship. But nowhere in his authentic
writings do we find the straightforward statements 'The
Holy Spirit is God' or 'The Holy Spirit is *homoousios*/
consubstantial with Father and Son.'

It is Gregory of Nazianzus who takes the plunge:
'What's this?' says his opponent, 'Is the Spirit God?' 'Certainly,' says Gregory. 'What's this?' says his opponent
again. 'Is it *homoousios*?' 'Yes,' replies Gregory, 'if it is

God.'[1] 'Furthermore,' he goes on (and here I am para-
phrasing), 'don't give me this nonsense about there being
only one possible relationship in the Trinity, that of begetter and begotten. The Holy Spirit is not created like a
creature, and it is not begotten like the Son. It *proceeds*, and
we know it proceeds because Christ himself says so in the
Gospel of John (Jn 15:26)!' It is true that Gregory is not too
sure of just *how* one 'proceeds' (it is incomprehensible, he
says, and we should not be so impertinent as to pry into
such matters), but then no one else was (or is) either. But
whatever it is and whatever it means, it is the distinguishing characteristic of the Holy Spirit: the Father is *ingenerate*
(he existed and has existed forever without origin or beginning); the Son is *generated* or *begotten* (but generated or
begotten eternally: we want no Arianism here); the Holy
Spirit *proceeds*. What is the difference between 'generation'
and 'procession'? 'I don't know,' says Gregory, 'but there
is one.'

The Cappadocians succeeded in their appointed task,
and the culmination of their endeavours may be seen in a
council held in Constantinople in 381. It was Theodosius I
who called the Council, and almost two hundred bishops
attended, all of them easterners. Yet despite the lack of
western representation, the Council was considered by
later theologians sufficiently momentous to be termed ecumenical, and it is therefore reckoned the Second Ecumenical Council of the universal church. Here the Nicene faith
finally triumphed; the term *homoousios* was formally
accepted of both the Son and the Spirit; the work of
Athanasius (dead now some eight years) found its fulfilment; and the Christian church recognized a doctrine of a
co-eternal and consubstantial Trinity, One and Three,
which, in its essence, has remained the accepted doctrine
ever since. Fifty-six years had elapsed since the process
had begun at the Council of Nicaea. Constantine had been

---

[1]Gregory of Nazianzus, *Oratio* 31, 10.

dead for more than forty years, and Basil the Great, who had done so much to make the Council possible, had died two years before it was convened.

And Arius himself? The originator of this long and convoluted controversy? After his condemnation and deposition at Nicaea, everyone forgot about him. He lived in banishment in Illyria (on the east coast of the Adriatic Sea); but round about 336, when he was in his eighties, sick and infirm, he pleaded with Constantine to permit him to take the sacraments before his death. Constantine agreed, and the traditional account (which may not be correct) of what happened afterwards is best described in the words of Edward Gibbon:

> On the same day which had been fixed for the triumph of Arius, he expired; and the strange and horrid circumstances of his death might excite a suspicion that the orthodox saints had contributed more efficaciously than by their prayers to deliver the church from the most formidable of her enemies.

And he adds the footnote:

> We derive the original story from Athanasius, who expresses some reluctance to stigmatise the memory of the dead. He might exaggerate; but the perpetual commerce of Alexandria and Constantinople would have rendered it dangerous to invent. Those who press the literal narrative of the death of Arius (his bowels suddenly burst out in a privy) must make their option between poison and miracle.[2]

---

[2]E. Gibbon (ed. O. Smeaton), *The Decline and Fall of the Roman Empire*, II: 285–286.

BASIL THE GREAT. Adapted from a fourth-century mosaic.

THE HOLY TRINITY. Adapted from the thirteenth-century minia-
ture. Christ, holding the Holy Spirit (represented by a dove),
sits on the lap of God the Father.

CHAPTER VII

THE WESTERN CONTRIBUTION

ALMOST ALL THE WRITERS and writings we have discussed so far have been Greek. The Council of Nicaea was conducted entirely in Greek and its creed and canons promulgated in Greek. Arius spoke Greek; Athanasius spoke Greek; the Cappadocians spoke Greek; and at the Second Ecumenical Council, held at Constantinople in 381, not a single westerner was present. In other words, the doctrine of the Trinity, as we have traced it so far, was almost entirely a product of Greek theologians. What, then, of the West? What had been going on in the Latin-speaking part of the Roman empire while the east was aflame with Arian and anti-Arian fire? The answer to this question depends on the area one is talking about: in the realms of ecclesiology (the doctrine of the church: what it is, what it should be, what it does) and certain aspects of sacramental theology, there were significant developments; but in the area on which we have been concentrating so far—the problems relating to the Trinity— the west contributed singularly little.

There was, certainly, Hippolytus (c. 170 – c. 235), but although his most important years were spent in Rome, Hippolytus himself was an immigrant. He had been born in the Greek-speaking east, and his native language (as well as the way he thought) was Greek. He was a learned and ambitious man, well versed in the philosophical systems of his day, and a voluminous writer, though much of his work has perished. His theology follows in direct line from that of Irenaeus of Lyons, Justin Martyr, and the Greek apologists: like them, he saw the Son as the revelation of the Father, and like them, too, he was undoubtedly subordinationist. But in his teaching he drew rather too clearly the line distinguishing the Father from the Son and was accused by two popes—Zephyrinus (198–217) and Callistus (217–222)—of being a Ditheist, someone who believed in two Gods. Hippolytus, as we might expect, wholly rejected this, and, in turn, accused his accusers of failing to make any clear distinction at all between the first and second persons of the Trinity. Furthermore, said Hippolytus, Zephyrinus is a greedy, weak, uneducated simpleton, and Callistus is an ex-convict (which was true: he had been imprisoned for embezzlement, though there are grounds for thinking he was innocent of the charge), who is also guilty of moral laxity. So incensed was Hippolytus, and so great was his dislike for Callistus, that when Zephyrinus died in 217 and Callistus was chosen as his successor, Hippolytus (so we are told, but the facts of the matter are not certain) refused to acknowledge him, set himself up in opposition, and thus became the first antipope in Christian history. The details of this unpleasant and acrimonious dispute need not here concern us, but we should notice that between them, Hippolytus, Zephyrinus, and Callistus were struggling with the same problem as so many of their eastern colleagues: just what is the relationship of Father and Son in a united Trinity, and how do we retain the oneness of God whilst distinguishing the persons?

Neither Zephyrinus nor Callistus was actually guilty of the doctrinal lapses of which they were accused by Hippolytus. They did not, in fact, confuse the Father and the Son, and what they were trying to do was to make it clear that although Christ the *Logos* was distinct from God the Father, there was still only one God; but that although there was only one God, he was not One Alone. Their intentions, in other words, were honourable; what they lacked was a suitably clear terminology in which to express them.

To find such a terminology we must move from Rome to the Roman province of North Africa, where, in about 160, was born Quintus Septimius Florens Tertullianus, by far the most brilliant of the pre-Nicene western theologians, and the first of them to write in Latin. Tertullian was a lawyer, not a philosopher; his training had been in rhetoric and law; and whereas Justin had thought of Socrates as a 'Christian before Christ,' Tertullian regarded him simply as a corruptor of young boys. 'What has Athens to do with Jerusalem?' he asks. 'What has Plato's Academy to do with the Church?' He has no time for 'Stoic Christianity' or 'Christian Platonism' and continually, time after time, lays stress on the Rule of Faith, the truth of the teaching of the church.

From the start it is clear that we are here in a thought-world very different from that of Justin or Irenaeus or Clement or Origen—or, for that matter, Hippolytus. The philosophical principles which left so decided a mark on pre-Nicene Greek thought are here absent, and although Tertullian cannot wholly divest himself of ideas which were, after all, imbibed with one's mother's milk and breathed in with every breath of air, there is no doubt that he has little time for the sometimes airy-fairy and ethereal philosophizing of his Greek contemporaries. He was a lawyer, and it was as a lawyer that he viewed the Christian situation. We are sinners and guilty; God is the just judge; and because he is just and we are guilty, we are condemned. Can anything be done? Indeed it can, and has been done already: Christ has paid our debt and has ransomed us, and Tertullian sees in the crucifixion the central and most important feature of Christianity. We do not achieve salvation by speculating on eternal generation and the term *homoousios*; we achieve salvation within the church through the death of Christ.

Tertullian was primarily a controversialist. He was not a systematic theologian. His violent spirit could ignite at any time, and his pen flame with ire and vituperation. He skillfully defends Christianity against the usual pagan misunderstandings; he sharply criticizes the polytheism of the Roman empire; he vigorously attacks the Gnostics and semi-Gnostics; he utterly condemns the games and spectacles in the arenas; he viciously lambasts women who use cosmetics and jewellery, and maintains that an interest in pretty clothes shows unwonted ambition and that the use of makeup betokens a whore. Yet amongst all this we find long and carefully argued passages, sometimes of great originality and brilliance, showing a true mastery both of Roman law and of the philosophy he affects to despise; and in two treatises in particular—one against Marcion and one against Praxeas—we find ideas and terminology which were to take on the first importance in Latin Christianity.

Marcion was a semi-Christian Gnostic, or semi-Gnostic Christian, who saw a total antipathy between the God of Love preached by Jesus of Nazareth in the New Testament and the vengeful, ignorant, and contradictory savage who dominated the Old Testament and whom the Jews worshipped. And since Marcion saw no relationship at all between the Old and New dispensations, he was not prepared to admit that the Messiah prophesied by the Jews could possibly have been Jesus of Nazareth. The Old Testament and the New; the God of Law and the God of Love; the Messiah and the Christ; the Jew and the Christian: they have nothing whatever in common.

Tertullian, naturally, rejects these views, and in his five books *Against Marcion* strives to demonstrate that Marcion's views are erroneous and that it is the direct opposite which is correct: the God of the two testaments is one and the same; there is no contradiction between them; and Christ is the true Messiah and truly human. Tertullian was

not, in fact, entirely successful in his endeavours: he had
no trouble in showing that Marcion was wrong, but he had
rather more difficulty in demonstrating that Christianity
was right; and in order to prove his point he had to rely
upon a considerable amount of high-flying allegorical exegesis (an approach which Marcion had rejected). But for all
that, his treatise is an intriguing work and is our main
source of information for the popular, persuasive, and
widely accepted ideas of Marcion himself.

In the case of Praxeas we are once more back in the realm
of Trinitarian thought. Praxeas seems to have come to
Rome from the east and arrived there towards the end of
the second century, and there is no doubt that he was
teaching doctrines which were as unacceptable to Christianity then as they are now. In his view, so far as we can
reconstruct it, the three persons of the Trinity had no real
and distinct existence. There was one God, who, at creation, *acted* as Creator; who, in the Incarnation, *acted* as the
Redeemer; and who, in inspiring the prophets and apostles, *acted* as the Holy Spirit. But these successive activities
lasted only so long as was needful, so that God the Son
existed as a separate manifestation of the one God only so
long as there was something for him to do. It is similar to
any one of us: at one and the same time we may be parent
(to a child), teacher (to a group of students), and customer
(in the local supermarket). But (a) there is only one of each
of us, not three; and (b) when we have finished our shop-
ping and returned home, we are no longer a customer.
These manifestations—these three ways in which we act—
are limited by place and time, and if we apply the analogy
to the Trinity, we see immediately that it is no Trinity at all.
There is no real and eternal distinction between Father,
Son, and Holy Spirit, and we have here not three distinct
and eternal realities, but three manifestations or activities
of one single reality. Hence, says Tertullian in a splendid
phrase, Praxeas has thrown out the Holy Spirit and crucified the Father. For if one of my students, incensed beyond

all bounds, takes out a pistol and shoots me, he shoots not only the teacher, but the customer and parent as well. Why? Because there is only *one* of me, not three, and the same is true of the God of Praxeas. It was for holding doctrines such as these that Hippolytus (unjustly) condemned Popes Zephyrinus and Callistus.

Tertullian will have none of this. He follows in the footsteps of Irenaeus of Lyons and maintains, firstly, that God was *always* three and one and that the three distinct realities of Father, Son, and Holy Spirit were *always* three distinct realities; and secondly, that in the unfolding of the divine plan—creation, incarnation, redemption, pentecost, and so on—each of these three realities is revealed separately and fully. In the incarnation, therefore, it is not just the one God 'acting' as Christ, but the truly distinct and eternal Son of God revealing himself in flesh at this moment in time. And by what name may we refer to these three realities? Here Tertullian takes advantage of the precision of Latin (we have seen all too much of the ambiguity of Greek) and establishes a terminology which was henceforth to be accepted as the standard terminology of the western church: there are three persons (*personae*) in one substance (*substantia*), and there is one God and one Trinity (*trinitas*: he is the first to use the term in this context).

These terms are not ambiguous. 'Person' can never mean 'substance,' and 'substance' can never mean 'person.' But as we have seen, the same was not true of the word *ousia* in Greek. It could mean either, and that is why the loaded term *homoousios* could imply 'same person' as well as 'same substance'; and if we maintain that Father, Son, and Holy Spirit are all the same *person*, we are back with the heresy of Praxeas. It was not until the time of the Cappadocian Fathers that Greek terminology became equally unambiguous, and we might say with some truth that if the Fathers at Nicaea had spoken in Latin and used the word 'consubstantial' rather than 'homoousios,' the work of Athanasius could have been reduced by half. It is no accident that in these pages I have used the terms 'substance' and 'person' throughout, even when speaking of the Greek east before such clarification existed. But without such unambiguous terminology, borrowed with thanks from Tertullian, any description of the complexities of the Arian crisis would become even more confusing than it already is.

Tertullian's contribution to Trinitarian doctrine was, however, primarily terminological. His understanding of the trinitarian relationships reflected the ideas of his times (the late second and early third century) and his sources (Justin and the other apologists), and he was, as we might expect, subordinationist. Although he recognizes that Father and Son share a common substance, he still believes they are different in degree. If the Father is the whole substance, the Son is only an outflow or derivation (*derivatio* in Latin), or a part or portion (*portio* in Latin), of the whole. But this, as we have seen, is standard pre-Nicene thinking, and we would hardly expect anything else.

Tertullian ended his days outside—or on the very fringes of—orthodoxy. In 207 he joined a movement known as Montanism. It had been founded by an obscure figure called Montanus (hence the name), and combined extremely rigorous ascetic demands with a belief in charismatic prophecy and the imminent arrival on earth of the Heavenly Jerusalem. And it was as a member of this movement that Tertullian died sometime after 220, although the precise year of his death is unknown. His contribution to western Christianity was considerable, not only for the terminology which he provided, but also for the way in which he stamped it with a certain character. The legalistic approach to the tradition; the stress on the Rule of Faith; the distrust—at least in theory—of philosophy; the emphasis on belief rather than speculation; all these appear first in Tertullian, and he is generally considered as one of the two outstanding Latin Christian writers of the patristic period. The other, of course, is the titan figure of Augustine of Hippo.

Tertullian's death came about a century before the Council of Nicaea, but despite the fact that thanks to him they had the necessary terminology to talk about the Trinity, the western theologians seemed disinclined to do so. There is no doubt that at the time the Arian controversy was raging in the east, many of the western bishops had only the vaguest understanding of what the fracas was all about, and a large number of them never saw a copy of the Nicene creed until years after the council. Many of them believed what it was politic for them to believe (we saw in the last chapter how chaotic were the events after 325); but in the years following Nicaea, as the Greek east slowly but inexorably leaned more and more towards the ideas of Athanasius, it pulled the Latin west along with it. To this tendency Athanasius himself made some contribution—many years of his exiles were spent in the west, not the east—and so, too, did the remarkable Hilary (c. 315–367), a convert from Later Platonism who became in due course bishop of Poitiers (in what is now central France). Hilary was a man quite at home in both worlds: he was as fluent in Greek as in Latin and as familiar with eastern ideas as with western ones. He became the leading Latin theologian of his day, and for his unwavering opposition to Arianism and his defence of the faith of Nicaea, he is often referred to as the 'Athanasius of the West.' Partly as a consequence of his efforts, partly as a consequence of the political situation, and partly as a consequence of the natural flow of ideas, western trinitarian thought in the post-Nicene period reflected that of the east; and after the Council of Constantinople in 381—the Second Ecumenical Council—the vast majority of Christians, of whatever language and whatever country, were prepared to acknowledge a consubstantial and co-eternal Trinity in which all three persons were co-eternally distinct, yet operated together as a unity.

The momentous and unique contribution which the west was to make to this doctrine would not occur until the early years of the following century, when the redoubtable Augustine developed what is known in technical theological jargon as the doctrine of the Double Procession of the Holy Spirit.

Augustine was born at Tagaste, in the Roman province of North Africa, in 354. His father was pagan, but his mother was deeply Christian and his early education was likewise Christian. He had originally intended to become a lawyer, but this ambition seems to have faded fairly rapidly, and from 373 his main interest lay in philosophy. Shortly after 373 he became a Manichaean—a creed he embraced for more than a decade—but eventually he abandoned it since it was manifestly unable to answer a number of fundamental questions which had been troubling him for years. He then moved to Rome, and from Rome to Milan, where he adopted the principles of Later Platonism and came under the influence of the acute and learned bishop of Milan, Ambrose. It was Ambrose who acted as the catalyst in Augustine's conversion, and at Easter in the year 387 he was baptized. The next year he returned to North Africa, where he was ordained priest in 391, and from this time onwards his influence and importance in the African church increased rapidly and dramatically. In 396 he was consecrated assistant bishop in the see of Hippo, and from the following year to his death in 430 he governed the diocese as sole bishop.

Augustine's impact on western Christian thought was immense —for many centuries the terms Western Christianity and Augustinian Christianity were simple synonyms—and in due course we shall be examining his ideas on sin, salvation, the church, and the sacraments. For the moment, however, our concern is with the Trinity, and as we said earlier, our immediate interest is the Augustinian doctrine of the Double Procession of the Holy Spirit, a doctrine which was to have widereaching political as well as theological ramifications and which was to establish a permanent distinction between the ways in which the east and the west viewed the threefold nature of God. What, then, is this doctrine, and how did it come about?

Perhaps the best way to appreciate it is by using some simple analogies: like all analogies, they cannot be pushed too far, but they may help to elucidate what is going on. Up to the time of Augustine—up to the early fifth century—both east and west had a very similar idea of how the Holy Spirit was produced: it proceeded (this, we may remember, is the official New Testament-Cappadocian term) *from* the Father *through* the Son. Tertullian illustrates this by using the analogy of a spring (= the Father) producing a river (= the Son), and a canal (= the Holy Spirit) being led off from the river; and if we take over this analogy and update it, then we can visualize the Father as an infinite reservoir of water, the Holy Spirit as the tap at which we drink, and the Son as the system of pipes and channels linking the two together. Or, if you prefer, the Holy Spirit is the electric socket in the wall; the Father is the power station; and the Son is the grid-system connecting the one with the other. In all these cases the third principle is channeled *through* the second principle *from* the first principle, and the theory is therefore referred to as *Single* Procession, since the Holy Spirit proceeds from the Father alone, and the Son merely does the 'channelling' or 'mediating' or 'transmitting.'

Now sometimes, when water travels through a series of pipes, it picks up certain chemicals or other materials from the pipes themselves. Thus, when we turn on the tap and fill up a glass, we get not only the pure water from the reservoir, but pure water *plus* the various additions which it has accumulated during its travels. Similarly, a number of theologians (Gregory of Nyssa, for example), maintained that the Spirit 'received from the Son' during the procession. Just what the Spirit received is not made clear, but what Gregory and the others wanted to imply was that in the process of the production of the Spirit, the Son was not just a passive agent, but did, in some wonderful way, make a positive contribution to the nature of the third person of the Trinity. Yet for all this, the eastern theologians—and those in the west up to the time of Augustine—remained loyal to the concept of Single Procession and to the two important prepositions, *from* and *through*.

Augustine's view of the Holy Spirit is radically different, and we must use a radically different analogy to explain it. Expressing it in human terms, Augustine says that the Father eternally generates the Son and that the Holy Spirit is not something which comes from the Father alone, but is the mutual love which Father and Son have for each other. In fact he goes further than this and says that the Holy Spirit is 'whatever is common' to Father and Son: e.g., their mutual love, mutual joy, mutual peace, mutual will, mutual happiness, mutual blessedness, mutual goodness, mutual charity, mutual delight, and anything else of this nature we care to name. But the problem with the human analogy is that we tend to think of Fathers and Sons as real and solid beings, and love as an amorphous and emotional something which is 'made' or 'fallen into' and which is synonymous with that curious phenomenon called 'lurve' which the pop stars sing about so incessantly. So a better analogy, perhaps, is that of an electric battery. Here we have *forces*, not people, and we can visualize the Father as the positive pole, the Son as the negative pole, and the Holy Spirit as the current flowing and flashing between them. Here we have only one substance (= electricity), and if the battery is to work, all three realities must be present and operating. You can no more get a current from a battery with one pole than you can lift yourself up by your own shoelaces. In the production of the electric current, both poles are essential and both have an *equal* part to play. To think of an eight-volt battery in which the positive pole produces seven volts and the negative produces one is ridiculous: the whole battery produces eight volts, and the two poles cooperate to precisely the same extent in producing the current.

This is how Augustine thought of the Holy Spirit. The infinite power which is the Father generates eternally the infinite power which is the Son (so they are consubstantial and co-eternal), and these two infinite powers eternally interact to produce the third infinite power which is the Holy Spirit. In other words, Augustine is not thinking of the procession of the Holy Spirit like this:

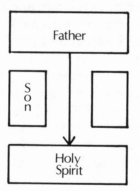

But like this:

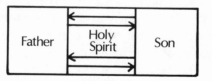

And since in this second scheme both Father and Son make *equal* contributions to the production of the Holy Spirit— the one is precisely as important as the other—the doctrine is referred to as Double Procession. Here the Holy Spirit proceeds not from the Father, THROUGH the Son, but from the Father AND the Son, and in later centuries this concept was to have profound political as well as theological consequences.

From the time of Augustine onwards the western church accepted this doctrine (and it still does); the eastern church did not (and it still doesn't). But both churches recognized a Trinity in which all three persons were consubstantial/*homoousios*, co-eternal, co-eternally distinct, and which operated as a unity. Since it was the three Cappadocian Fathers who finally managed to get this view accepted, we may refer to it as 'Cappadocian orthodoxy.' So from the end of the fourth century, the eastern churches have had a doctrine of the Trinity which can be summarized as 'Cappadocian orthodoxy with Single Procession,' and since the time of Augustine the western churches have had a doctrine of 'Cappadocian orthodoxy with Double Procession.' And that is how it has remained ever since.

CRUCIFIXION. Adapted from a fifth-century ivory casket.

CHAPTER VIII

CHRIST: BODY AND SOUL

B Y THE END OF THE FOURTH CENTURY the Christian world was either convinced or well on its way to being convinced that Christ the *Logos*, the second person of the Trinity, was truly God and truly divine. But what happened when this divine *Logos* became incarnate? How did the Godhead combine or conjoin or unite with the manhood in the single person of Jesus of Nazareth? Was he a man in whom God dwelt? Or was he merely a man inspired by God? Or was he a man who *was* God? What was it that Mary bore?

To answer these questions we must first travel back in history from the time of the Cappadocian Fathers to that of the Apostolic Fathers and investigate what they had to say upon the matter. Their concern lay almost entirely with demonstrating the *reality* of Christ's incarnation—that he was real flesh and blood—for there was a pronounced tendency among some Christian, and particularly Gnostic Christian, communities of their era to deny this fact and maintain instead that Christ only *appeared* to be human. At the root of this idea lurked Later Platonism, with its hierarchy of being. As we pointed out in Chapter II, the view of the Platonists was that the further down the scale

91

you descended—from the One to the Divine Mind to the World-Soul to the world—the worse things became, and this conception had been exaggerated by the Gnostic sects, who, by interposing large numbers of aeons or intermediaries between the Supreme Being and this world, had utterly removed the one from the other and saw created stuff—rock, flesh, wood, blood, or what have you—as straightforwardly evil. For these Gnostics and Platonic Christians, there was very little (if anything) good about flesh and bone and blood, and they were quite unable to understand how a truly good Being—i.e., Christ the *Logos*—could possibly be united with something truly bad or imperfect—i.e., human flesh. It would be like saying that white could be black or a square could be a circle. The thing was obviously impossible.

Their solution to the problem was simple: Christ did not *become* man, but only *appeared* to be a man. His humanity was an illusion, an appearance: his disciples and everyone else thought he was real, but this was not the case. They were like the audience in a 3–D movie, mistaking the figure on the screen for a real person, responding to him, talking to him, learning from him, and failing to realize that what they took for reality was not reality at all, but simply an ever-changing pattern of beams of light. And since the Greek word for an 'appearance' was *dokētos*, this view became known as *docetism*, or 'appearance-ism.'

To this view the Apostolic Fathers (together with the Apologists and their successors) objected in the strongest possible terms. And quite rightly. Docetism spells disaster for Christianity, and an unreal Saviour can only produce an unreal salvation. If Christ's humanity were an illusion, his suffering and death on Calvary were an illusion; if his suffering and death were an illusion, his resurrection was an illusion; and if his humanity, suffering, death, and resurrection were an illusion, the redemption of the human race was also an illusion. In other words, if Christ's flesh were not true flesh, then we are still in our sins.

For many of the Gnostics this was not of any great consequence. Their view of the matter was that salvation was achieved by knowledge, not by the crucifixion, and their Christ was a Christ who revealed passwords and Gnostic truth, not a Christ who came to die. It made no difference to them, therefore, whether Christ was truly human or not, just as it makes no difference to us whether we are taught geography by a human teacher in the classroom or by a videotape at home. But this was never the orthodox Christian view: for the Christians, Christ died for our sins, and you cannot kill a videotape.

As a consequence of such arguments as these, and as a consequence of the decay of Gnosticism in the course of the third century, docetism gradually became of less and less importance, and by the end of the pre-Nicene period it was generally accepted among Christians that the flesh and blood and sufferings of Jesus of Nazareth were real flesh and blood and sufferings and that the salvation of humanity could only be achieved by a truly human saviour. But if the flesh was indeed true flesh, how was it animated? What made it work and walk and talk? In ordinary human beings it was the soul which was seen as the animating agent, and the Christian world defined death simply as the separation of soul and body. The most obvious suggestion, therefore, was that just as an ordinary human being is flesh and blood animated by a rational soul, the incarnate Christ was flesh and blood animated by God the Son, the second person of the Trinity. It is just like slipping a letter into an envelope or filling a bottle with wine or wrapping a candy in paper: you take the body born of Mary on the one hand and Christ the *Logos* on the other, slip the latter into the former, and lo and behold! we have the incarnate Christ in the person of Jesus of Nazareth. And it was this simple and straightforward way of regarding the incarnation which dominated Christian thought from its beginnings to some fifty years after the Council of Nicaea.

Enter Apollinaris, bishop of Laodicea. Born about 310, he became in due course a close friend of Athanasius and a staunch defender of the faith of Nicaea. He was consecrated bishop of Laodicea (a city on the coast of present-day Syria, just opposite Cyprus) in about 360, and as an orthodox bishop of an important diocese, Apollinaris (or Apollinarius, as he is also—and less accurately—called) was in no doubt that Christ the *Logos* was truly God and truly divine and that Jesus of Nazareth was truly real and truly human. But unfortunately for Apollinaris, he also considered that the best way of expressing the real unity of God and man in the incarnate Christ was by maintaining (with some development) what had been maintained for centuries: that in Christ, the divine *Logos* simply took the place of the human soul. If this were not the case, he thought, and if, in Christ, there was a human soul as well as the divine *Logos*, then (1) we would make Christ into a sort of schizophrenic or a dual personality, and (2) we would be maintaining that in God Incarnate there existed the possibility of sin and moral progress.

It is, after all, the human soul of a human being which feels pain, develops morally, and faces temptation. You can prove this quite easily by finding a cadaver (let us say at the local undertaker's), sticking a pin in its toe, and then inviting it to have a drink, a cigarette, or to look at a blue movie, depending on its preferences in life. Nothing happens. It is not the flesh—the meat—which feels pain and temptation, but the flesh animated by a rational soul, and Apollinaris was not prepared to admit that there was such a soul in Christ. Christ was the incarnate *God*, and God cannot feel pain, God cannot be tempted, and God does not make moral progress as we do. Christ, said Apollinaris, is 'God enfleshed' or 'God bearing flesh' (they are some of his favourite terms), and in Jesus of Nazareth there is neither need nor place for a human soul.

Furthermore, said Apollinaris, as a result of this intimate fusion of the divine *Logos* and human flesh, the nature of the flesh is to some extent transformed. Christ, after all, is not two people—*Logos* and flesh—but one. Apollinaris is no dualist. There is 'one nature of the Word of God enfleshed,' and so intimate is the union that the properties of divinity are communicated, to some extent, to the flesh with which it is united. Using the analogy we used earlier: if you write a letter on perfumed paper and then slip it into an envelope and seal it, the envelope absorbs the scent and itself becomes redolent. In just the same way, the flesh of Christ became 'divine flesh' or 'God's flesh,' and therefore capable of certain actions which are not normally possible for ordinary human beings. It could walk on water, for example, or be transfigured, or survive death. And Apollinaris took these ideas to their logical conclusion by maintaining that in the eucharist, too, the bread becomes not just the flesh but the *divine* flesh of Christ and that when the believers partake of this bread/flesh, they are 'deified' or 'divinized' by so doing. Christ's flesh, imbued with the divine powers of God the *Logos*, actually communicates divinity to those who consume it.

This concept of the incarnation had a long previous history. Apollinaris develops the idea further than his predecessors, that is true, but there is no doubt that he was building on a well-established tradition. Unfortunately, as we have seen before (most notably in the case of Arius), ideas which were acceptable at one time may not be acceptable at another, and the views of Apollinaris, which might have caused no comment half a century earlier, became the target of determined attack in the late fourth century by those energetic and capable defenders of orthodoxy, the Cappadocian Fathers.

Their objections were essentially threefold: firstly, if the flesh of Christ is 'divine flesh,' then it is not ordinary human flesh; and if it is not ordinary human flesh, then what is it? It is an easy step to say, 'No, it isn't ordinary human flesh; it only *appears* to be so.' But if we say that, we teeter on the brink of docetism, and it was well known by this time that docetism was not a viable Christian alternative.

Secondly, just what *is* a real human being? Surely, said the Christians (and almost everyone else west of India), a human being is body plus soul, and the truly human thing about a truly human being is not the meat and sinew and muscle and blood and bone—the birds and animals have that—but the rational human soul. Furthermore, there is a wealth of evidence in the New Testament which shows that Christ *was* subject to human emotions and passions— he got angry, he was sad, he rejoiced, he wept—and since God the *Logos* is, by definition, exempt from such feelings and emotions, and since human flesh, dead or unanimated, is good for nothing (even eating it is considered bad form), then the only thing that could possibly feel these emotions is the human soul. In other words, if we believe that Christ was truly human, and if we believe the New Testament, then we must also believe that a human soul was an integral part of his constitution. In any case, says Gregory of Nazianzus, what could be clearer evidence than the agony in the garden of Gethsemane? Here we have a superb example of conflict between the human soul and the divine *Logos*: 'Father, let this cup pass from me,' says the human soul; 'but thy will be done,' says the divine *Logos*. And so great was the agony, say some versions of Luke, that his sweat became mixed with blood.

The third argument is the most important, but it is also the most theological, and to understand it we must go back in time to the letters of Paul and to the writings of the apologist Irenaeus of Lyons. According to Paul, 'just as in Adam all die, so also in Christ shall all be made alive' (1 Cor 15:22), and later in the same letter he contrasts the first Adam—Adam—with the second or last Adam—Christ (1 Cor 15:45–50). This parallelism is much elaborated by Irenaeus in a doctrine conveniently referred to as 'recapitulation,' a word which means literally 'summing up all previous events.' Irenaeus contrasts the first Adam and all that he did with the second Adam and all that he did, and shows how the obedience, sinlessness, and perfection of the latter (= Christ) has cancelled out the disobedience, sinfulness, and imperfection of the former (= Adam) and that in the incarnation we therefore see the beginning of the new and restored creation. It is just like the two pans of a balance: in the left-hand pan we put Adam; in the right-hand pan, Christ. In the left, Adam's disobedience; in the right, Christ's obedience. In the left, Adam's sin; in the right, Christ's lack of sin. And so on. Everything we put in the one pan must be counter-balanced by what goes in the other, for everything which went wrong in Adam has been put right in Christ.

It is this doctrine which forms the basis for the arguments of the Cappadocians, and there are three essential points which follow from it. (1) Christ, in the right-hand pan, must balance Adam in the left. But of what did Adam consist? Unquestionably, he consisted of body *AND SOUL*. Therefore, if the one is to balance the other, Christ must also have a body *AND SOUL*. (2) If Adam was truly tempted and fell, Christ must also have been truly tempted, yet did not fall. But as we explained earlier, the unchangeable God cannot be tempted, and you cannot tempt inanimate flesh. It is the *human soul* which is tempted and which utilizes the flesh to satisfy these temptations. If, then, Christ was really tempted (and Matthew 4:1 says that he was: 'Then Jesus was led into the desert by the Spirit, to be tempted by the Devil'), he must have had a temptable soul. But if, on the other hand, he was *not* really tempted (and the Christ of Apollinaris is, essentially, untemptable), then he could claim no credit for not having fallen, and we have put nothing in the right-hand pan of the balance to cancel out what we have put in the left. My cat, for example, has been castrated, and therefore gains no credit for living a disciplined and celibate life. Similarly, you cannot blame someone with no hands for not catching a ball, or praise someone with two legs for being bipedal. (3) The sin of Adam affected not only his body —which became mortal and subject to death, disease, and corruption—but also his soul—which developed a tendency to wickedness and became stained and tainted with sin. All humanity, therefore, has contracted these problems, and all humanity has been corrupted in both soul and body. It follows, then, that if we are to be redeemed fully, we must be redeemed in both soul and body, and for that to occur, both soul and body must have been present in Christ. As Adam's body became subject to death, Christ's body triumphed over death: and as we died in Adam, so we shall live in Christ. As Adam's soul became stained with sin, Christ's soul was pure and sinless, and in and through Christ we are offered forgiveness of sins and life everlasting. But as Gregory of Nazianzus said: 'What was not assumed, was not healed.' If Christ did not assume true flesh, our flesh has not been redeemed; if he did not assume a true human soul, then our souls, and therefore we, are still in our sins. Half a redemption is no good to anyone.

There are, in fact, certain problems with this doctrine of recapitulation—the most obvious being that if Adam = body + soul, but Christ = body + soul + *Logos*, there is already an imbalance—but there seems little doubt that the arguments and efforts of the Cappadocians met with great success and wide acceptance. They were not the first to voice their suspicions of Apollinaris' theories (the same or very similar views had already been condemned at the Council of Alexandria in 362), but their prestige, authority, and theological skill ensured that its downfall was more rapid and more complete. Apollinarianism was condemned at a series of councils held between 378 and 381, and in a number of decrees issued between 383 and 388, Theodosius I, the emperor who had already outlawed Arianism, also placed Apollinarianism, too, beyond the pale of the law. By this time Apollinaris himself had left the church, but of his later years nothing is known, and he died in obscurity in about 390.

We may say, then, that by the end of the third century docetism was generally recognized to be unacceptable and the majority of orthodox Christians were agreed that the flesh of Christ was real; and that by the end of the fourth century, Apollinarianism had been condemned and the majority of orthodox Christians were agreed that Christ also had a human soul. The question which must now engage our attention is just how this true humanity was united with the true divinity, and precisely what terminology was best suited to express it. To deal with this we must move on in time from the fourth century to the fifth, take a very deep breath, and immerse ourselves, with some trepidation, in one of the most complex and confusing controversies ever to trouble the Christian world.

Cyril of Alexandria. Adapted from a sixteenth-century greek
icon.

CHAPTER IX

CHRIST: GOD AND MAN

T O UNDERSTAND MORE EASILY just what was going on in the great Christological controversy we may find it helpful to make three preliminary points, for if we have no landmarks to guide us in this complex matter we will appreciate neither where we stand nor where we are trying to go. The first point involves the distinction between *confusion* of natures and *separation* of natures, for these represent the two unacceptable extremes between which we must steer a difficult middle course. By 'natures' we mean the two natures which were united in the single person of Jesus of Nazareth: the nature of the godhead (= the second person of the Trinity, God the *Logos*, consubstantial and co-eternal with the Father and Holy Spirit) and the nature of the manhood (= the flesh born of Mary, animated by a rational human soul). In other words, the two natures are the full and perfect divinity on the one hand and the full and perfect humanity on the other.

What, then, do we mean by 'confusion' of these two natures, and why is it unacceptable? As usual, an analogy may be useful: let us symbolize the divinity by whisky and the humanity by water and mix them one with the other. The result? Whisky-and-water: a drink in which the non-

alcoholic nature of the water has been made alcoholic by
the admixture of the whisky, and the strength of the
whisky has been diluted by the admixture of the water
(though this is not a part of the analogy I wish to stress).
Furthermore, once the two are mixed together it is impossible to separate them (we are in a pub, not a laboratory),
and again, since the whole of the liquid is now alcoholic,
we may easily make the mistake of attributing to the
whisky the properties of water and to the water the properties of whisky. We could thus be led to spend the rest of our
lives drinking water and washing in whisky, which would
leave us sober but bankrupt. Let us now apply this analogy
to the incarnation: if the divinity and humanity are mixed
in this way, the humanity is transformed by the fusion (the
water becomes alcoholic), and thereby loses its true nature.
It is no longer human as we are human, and a non-human
Saviour cannot save the human race. Furthermore, as a
consequence of the fusion we may be led to assert of
divinity what should only be asserted of humanity, and of
humanity what should only be asserted of divinity. We
may thus be tempted to speak of an eternal man or a
weeping Godhead, or to suggest that when Christ, on the
cross, cried out, 'My God, my God, why hast thou for-
saken me?' he was talking to himself. 'Confusion of natures,' therefore, or 'confused union' leads to a denial of
Christ's human-ness and to the theologically unacceptable
idea that God the *Logos* felt pain, or that the second person
of the Trinity, the immutable and unchangeable Wisdom of
God, grew in wisdom (Luke 2:40). The idea is wholly
illogical and cannot be accommodated within the Christian
tradition. God has neither parts nor passions, and the
Fathers knew from the letter of James (1:17) that in Him
there was neither change nor variation.

What, then, of 'separation' of natures? Here we go to the
opposite extreme and maintain that no real union has
taken place at all. Here we may symbolize the divinity by a
square block of black ebony and the humanity by a square

block of light pine: we carefully place one block on top of the other, and that is all there is to it. There is certainly no confusion here—you can see the dark wood and the light wood without the slightest difficulty—but nor is there any real uniting. One block is just resting on the other (it is not even glued to it) and may be removed at any time. If we now apply this to the incarnation, we see that Christ is not 'the God-man'—a true union of divinity and humanity— but 'God-with-man' or 'God-resting-on-man,' and that is to imply that Christ is no more than a prophet. The prophets were people on whom God 'rested' for a while, thereby inspiring them, but no one ever called a prophet 'God incarnate.' If you will permit another analogy, they were like modern teenagers walking around with their transistor radios close to their ears: what the radio transmits to them is what they say. Or like Long John Silver with his parrot on his shoulder: 'Pieces of eight,' whispers the parrot into Long John's ear, and 'pieces of eight' is what Long John prophesies. In none of these cases—the two blocks of wood, transistor and teenager, parrot and pirate—is there any real uniting of the one thing with the other, and to apply the principle to Jesus of Nazareth is to transform him simply into a man inspired by God, a super-prophet, but not the incarnate *Logos*. And since no prophet ever did or could bring about the redemption of the human race, a Christ in whom the divine and human natures are separated is of no use to Christianity.

Where, then, do we go from here? If we must neither 'confuse' nor 'separate' the natures, how are we to understand the incarnation? The answer lies in the paradoxical expression 'unconfused union,' a phrase which is intended to imply (1) that a real personal uniting of God and man has taken place, but (2) that in this uniting, the characteristics and properties of both natures are preserved entire and intact. Here we have *distinction* of natures, but not separation, and *uniting* of natures, but not confusion. To find an analogy for this conception is, of course, ultimately impossible, and the best I can do is to symbolize the divinity by light-coloured sand and the humanity by dark-coloured sand, and mix them together. The resultant material now *appears* to be grey, but if we look at it very closely and very carefully we can still see the individual grains of dark and light sand, and we can also see that not one of them has changed in colour. Furthermore, for all practical purposes, we cannot now separate the millions of grains back into their constituent colours, even though we can discern them. So what we have here is something which *appears* to be confused, but is not, and something in which the two constituents retain their individual characteristics—dark and light—but cannot be separated once they have been joined together. In other words, we have an *unconfused union*, and that, as we shall see in due course, is the only tolerable Christian alternative.

So much, then, for the first general point we need to make. It is certainly the most important of the three, and must be kept in mind throughout all the discussion which follows. The other two are rather simpler: one is geographical and theological, and the other geographical and political. The former involves Alexandria and Antioch; the latter, Alexandria and Constantinople.

As we saw in Chapter IV, at the end of the second century there developed in Alexandria a famous Catechetical School of which the greatest teachers were Clement of Alexandria and Origen. We also observed in the same chapter how too great a dependence on Later Platonic thought could lead to an over-emphasis on the spiritual to the detriment of the temporal, or, in the case of Christ, to too great an emphasis on the divinity at the expense of the humanity. Since Alexandrian theology was also Christian-Platonist theology, it will not come as a surprise to find that this emphasis on the divine was one of the most characteristic features of the teaching of the school. Apollinaris, whom we met in the last chapter, was Alexandrian in his theology, and we have seen how his over-emphasis on the divinity of Christ led to a denial of his true humanity (he had no human soul), and how Apollinaris' insistence on the completeness of the union of *Logos* and flesh led to the idea of 'divine flesh,' of a sharing of divine and human properties, or, in other words, of confusing the natures.

The other side of the theological coin was represented by Alexandria's rival: the Catechetical School of Antioch. Whereas Alexandria was always more Greek, more hellenistic, in its views, and leaned always to the mystical and allegorical, to the delights of philosophical and spiritual speculation, Antioch was always more down-to-earth and practical. Its theology looked more to Judaea than to Greece, more to the semitic soul than to the hellenistic, and the practical common sense so characteristic of semitic thinking may clearly be seen in the Antiochene stress on the literal and historical meaning of scripture (not the mystical and the allegorical), and in its emphasis on the humanity of Jesus of Nazareth, sometimes at the expense of his divinity. The Antiochenes therefore stressed the *distinction* of the natures in Christ: he was man and he was God; the Alexandrians stressed the *union* of the natures: he was 'the God-man,' God incarnate. The Antiochenes stressed the features of his true humanity: he rejoiced, wept, suffered, and died; the Alexandrians stressed the features of his true divinity: he was God from God, light from light, consubstantial and co-eternal, the divine *Logos*, God made man. It is clear, too, that if we push Antiochene thought to its extreme, the stress on distinction of natures all too easily becomes *separation*; and if we push Alexandrian thought to its extreme, the stress on the unity all too easily leads to *confusion*.

Our third and final point is somewhat more political. We noted in Chapter V that at the Council of Nicaea certain decrees (canons) were promulgated which ranked the great metropolitan sees in order of precedence. The first in order was Rome, the second Alexandria, the third Antioch, and the others need not concern us. But this Council was held in 325, five years before Constantine officially inaugurated Constantinople as his new imperial capital, and later councils therefore had to decide what to do about the new imperial city. The result was never really in doubt: to the extreme displeasure of Alexandria, which had hitherto been the most important eastern diocese, Constantinople shouldered its way into the space between Alexandria and Rome, called itself the 'New Rome,' relegated Alexandria to third place in the diocesan order, and arrogated for itself preeminence in the east. It is easy to understand, then, that from the end of the fourth century, when this rearrangement occurred, there was often rivalry and antagonism between the bishops of the two great cities, and certain patriarchs of Alexandria were not averse to using the most unethical and devious tactics to secure the deposition of their hated rivals in the imperial see.

With these interminable, though essential, preliminary comments behind us, we may now introduce Nestorius. Born sometime in the later fourth century he was trained in Antioch (note!), and gained a great reputation as a preacher. When the see of Constantinople became vacant in the year 428, Nestorius was appointed as bishop. Like the owner of a new house, the new bishop was eager to clean in all the corners, and this, in theological terms, meant getting rid of those who held heretical, unorthodox, or dangerous opinions. He therefore supported his chaplain, Anastasius, when the latter proclaimed that the use of the title *Theotokos* for the Virgin Mary smacked of Apollinarianism. We must therefore pause to inquire into the meaning of this title and investigate just why it might imply the heretical —and condemned—views of Apollinaris.

First of all, what does *Theotokos* mean? It is derived from two Greek words, *theos* 'god' and *tokos* 'a bringing forth, a birth,' and the two together—*Theotokos*—mean 'one who brings forth God.' It is usually translated 'God-bearer' and is the Greek equivalent of the Latin *Mater Dei* or *Dei*

Genetrix, 'Mother of God.' The title had been used of Mary from the third century —perhaps even from the second— and by the fifth century was universally accepted and widely used.

Secondly, of what was Apollinaris accused? He was accused of denying the true humanity of Christ and asserting that because of the fusion of divinity and humanity, the flesh of Christ became divine. In other words, he was accused of confusing the natures.

Thirdly, how does the first point lead to the second? Consider: was the eternal Godhead ever an infant two or three months old? Not in any literal sense. Does God have a mother? Not in any literal sense. Did the second person of the Trinity, the divine Light, wet his bed and make a mess in his diapers? This is clearly no simple question, and we might prefer to avoid it. But if we confuse the natures, we *can* say these things (look back at the very beginning of this chapter); and conversely, if we say these things, we might be implying confusion of natures. What Anastasius and Nestorius said, therefore, was that *Theotokos* or 'Mother of God' was a dangerous term to use, and Nestorius (a good Antiochene, remember, who consequently emphasized the *distinction* of the godhead and the manhood) suggested that if it was to be used, it should be used only in combination with *anthrōpotokos*, which means 'man-bearer.' And if 'Mary the God-bearer and man-bearer' should prove too much of a mouthful, then the easiest and neatest way out is surely to avoid both and refer to Mary simply and precisely as *Christotokos*, or 'Christ-bearer.' Furthermore, said Nestorius, just to be on the safe side, it might also be wiser to avoid the term 'union' when speaking of the Godhead and manhood in Christ: the word might possibly imply some confusion of the natures. It might be better to speak of the 'conjunction' of humanity and divinity, since two things 'conjoined' are less likely to be thought of as 'mixed up' or 'amalgamated' or—God forbid!—'confused.' In summary, then, according to the bishop of Constantinople, (1) *Theotokos* is a dangerous term and best avoided; and (2) 'union' is a dangerous term, and 'conjunction' is better.

It should be added here that Nestorius was not the first to stress the distinction of natures in the incarnate Christ. His ideas and, indeed, his terminology had been anticipated by two earlier Antiochenes: Diodore, the bishop of Tarsus (a most learned man who wrote a large number of treatises, but whose work survives only in fragments), and Theodore, bishop of Mopsuestia (the modern town of Misis in southern Turkey, about twenty miles east of Adana). Theodore was Diodore's pupil, and both bishops objected most strongly to the views of Apollinaris, whose ultra-Alexandrian ideas we discussed in the last chapter. Both, therefore, insisted on the presence of a human rational soul in Christ, but both, as staunch Antiochenes, likewise insisted that the human soul and the divine *Logos* must not, under any circumstances, be confused. In Diodore's case it seems that the stress on distinction may indeed have come dangerously close to separation, but it is difficult to be certain of this because of the very fragmentary condition of his once voluminous writings. But in Theodore's case, with more material to work from, we may see an excellent example of a devout and orthodox Antiochene attempting, with all his skill, to unite the natures in Christ without confusing them, and to distinguish between them without bringing about their separation. The precise details of Theodore's christology are still not wholly clear (and it is beyond the scope of this brief study to attempt to disentangle them), but what seems certain is that despite his good intentions, the language and terminology he used to express his ideas were somewhat perilous and were certainly open to misinterpretation. On the other hand, no one seems to have noticed this during his lifetime, and when Theodore died in 428 he died as an esteemed and respected bishop of the orthodox church. But when Nestorius died some twenty-three years later, he died as a heretic, deposed and in exile. Why? For two main reasons: firstly, because Mopsuestia was not Constantinople and the bishop of Mopsuestia was not the foremost prelate of the eastern Christian world; and secondly, Theodore did not have for his opponent the formidable Cyril, the brilliant but devious bishop of Alexandria, whom we must now introduce upon the stage.

Cyril was a man of acute intellect, but violent passions, and detested alike the heretics, the Jews, the Later Platonists (he certainly bears some of the responsibility for the brutal murder of the philosopher Hypatia, a distinguished and learned woman, who was torn to pieces by a Christian mob in Alexandria in 415), and, above all, Nestorius. As bishop of Alexandria he disliked Nestorius as bishop of Constantinople (that upstart and interfering see); as an Alexandrian theologian he disliked him as an Antiochene; and as Cyril he loathed him as Nestorius. He and his party therefore began to spread the rumour—partly, perhaps, from misunderstanding, but also partly from malice—that Nestorius would not call Mary 'Mother of God' because he did not believe that Jesus was God. For if Mary is not 'Mother of God,' what is she mother of? The answer is obvious: she is just the mother of a man, an ordinary human child just like any one of us, who was then 'adopted' by God or 'taken over' by God or 'entered' by God or 'inspired' by God, and thereby transformed into Christ. This, clearly, is to class Christ with the prophets—they, too, were ordinary men 'inspired' by God (i.e., we have separated the natures)—and to deny one of the basic presuppositions of the Christian faith: *viz.*, that Jesus of Nazareth was God incarnate, and was God incarnate from his conception.

Cyril, therefore, became the champion of the *Theotokos*, the most vociferous defender of the term, maintaining again and again that if you are unsure of the title, you are likewise unsure of the divinity of Christ. Christ was God from his conception, true God and true man, and if Nestorius thinks otherwise (which, we might add, he did not), then he is a heretic and no Christian. Cyril also objected to Nestorius' use of the term 'conjunction.' For Nestorius, it was the safest term to use, since 'union' could so easily imply confusion, and although he occasionally does use the word 'union,' he was not especially happy in doing so. Cyril looks at the matter from quite the opposite point of view: 'conjunction' implies *separation* of natures; it is 'union' which is safe! 'Conjoining' implies nothing more than a loose bond, an incidental relationship, and is only to be expected from someone like Nestorius, who, as everyone knew, was an Antiochene heretic who disbelieved in the divinity of Christ. How do you tell orthodox Christians from the other variety? By listening to their language. If they freely and happily use the terms *Theotokos* and 'union,' they are orthodox; if they do not, suspect the worst.

Now it is easy—too easy—in this exchange to see Nestorius as the wholly innocent party and Cyril as his evil demon: to see Nestorius as the spotless lamb of Constantinople devoured by the fury of the Alexandrian dragon. Such a view would be unfair and inaccurate, for although the intentions of Nestorius were good, his actions lacked tact, his language was often provocative and incautious, and in his description of the linkage of the Godhead and manhood in Christ, he used terms with the most unfortunate implications. The conjunction, he said (following Theodore of Mopsuestia), was 'according to *eudokia*,' a Greek word which could be translated as 'by grace, favour, good pleasure, or good will,' and whatever Nestorius (and Theodore) meant by it (and that is not altogether clear), there is no doubt that this is also the way God dwells in or with his prophets and saints. But if Christ is no more than a super-prophet or maxi-saint, Nestorius has separated the natures and has denied the possibility of salvation. Nestorius, of course, never intended this, and never, at any time, denied Christ's divinity, but his terminology was unquestionably unsound, and Cyril, who, despite his other faults, was a first-class theologian, was perfectly correct in castigating it.

On the other hand, Nestorius never ever said that Jesus was a mere man, nor did he refuse to use the title *Theotokos*, and Cyril's presentation of his views was, without doubt, maliciously exaggerated.

Throughout 430, in a series of important letters (the second and third Synodical Epistles) and dogmatic treatises, Cyril worked for the downfall of Nestorius, and late in that year, the emperor Theodosius II (who was the grandson of Theodosius I, and a man as genuinely pious as he was politically incompetent) summoned a council to meet in Ephesus at Pentecost in 431. He had realized the seriousness of the controversy and hoped to settle it at this synod, but his hopes, inevitably, were doomed to disappointment. The council—called, regrettably, the Third Ecumenical Council—was a farce. Nestorius' main supporters—John, bishop of Antioch (note!) and his colleagues—were delayed in their voyage to Ephesus, so Cyril opened the proceedings without them. Nor did he wait for the representatives from Rome, who would, in any case, have supported him. The conclusions of the council were therefore wholly predictable: Nestorius was condemned and excommunicated; and when John of Antioch and the pro-Nestorian party arrived four days later, they found that what they had come to discuss had already been decided and that the whole business had been concluded. This, understandably, caused them some irritation, so John and his colleagues immediately held their own synod, examined the case in their own way, and came up with a result just as predictable as that of their rival council: it was Cyril who was condemned and excommunicated, and the emperor was faced with an absurd situation. He had hoped that Ephesus would put an end to the controversy; but instead it had produced two excommunicated patriarchs, and the intolerable situation of an irresistible force (= Alexandria) meeting an immoveable object (= Constantinople). Theodosius had further problems within his own household: he had always been a weak man, but had the misfortune to be associated with two very strong women: his elder sister Pulcheria and his wife Eudokia. When we learn that the former supported Cyril and the latter supported Nestorius, we can only sympathize with an emperor whose home life, religious life, and political life were all alike in chaos.

At this point Theodosius imprisoned both Cyril and Nestorius while he decided what to do, but during his time in prison, the indefatigable Cyril, by a little persuasion and a great deal of bribery, enticed a considerable number of influential people into the anti-Nestorian camp. Nestorius, at this stage, realized what was happening and seems to have lost heart and given up the struggle. He wanted nothing more to do with the matter and requested that he be allowed to return to Antioch, there to enter the monastery in which he had been trained and end his days in peace. Part of his wish was granted: he was indeed permitted to go back to his monastery, but only for a few years. In 435 Theodosius banned his books, and in 436 he was banished to a remote oasis far in the south of Egypt, and there, in obscurity, he died shortly after 451.

Nestorius' retirement from the fray still left certain difficulties unresolved: primarily the rift between Cyril and John of Antioch. The emperor was demanding that something be done about this important matter, and Cyril, now that Nestorius had gone, could afford to be a little more lenient. In fact, he was forced to be very lenient indeed, and although both sides in the dispute had no choice but to compromise, it was Cyril who had to compromise more. In

433 he and John signed the so-called *Formula of Reunion*, which stated, amongst other things, that Christ was:

> the only-begotten Son of God, perfect God and perfect man, of a rational soul and body, before the ages begotten from the Father in his divinity; and the same in the last days . . . [begotten] from Mary the Virgin in his humanity, consubstantial (*homoousios*) with us in his humanity; for there has come to be a union of two natures, and we therefore confess one Christ, one Son, one Lord. On account of this idea of unconfused union, we confess the Holy Virgin to be *Theotokos*, because God the Word became flesh and became human, and from the very conception united to himself the temple (i.e., the body) which he took from her.

We must pay careful heed to the language of this document, for the terms used are loaded terms and cannot be appreciated without an understanding not only of the Nestorian controversy, but also of the Arian and Apollinarian controversies which preceded it: 'of a rational soul and body,' 'begotten from the Father,' '*homoousios*,' 'union of two natures,' 'unconfused union,' '*Theotokos*,' 'became flesh and became human,' 'from the very conception.'

By signing this document, John and Cyril established an uneasy peace which was to last for some fifteen years. But because of the compromises involved (and as we might expect, the hard-liners on both sides had no time for any compromise), it was a peace which was insecurely based and was doomed eventually to be overthrown. The great controversy was dormant, but not ended, and as we shall see in the next chapter, when it flared up again, it flared up to even greater heights than it had attained before.

In a chapter such as this, it is easy to lose one's way among the political intrigues and double-dealing and fail to see what lay at the heart of the Christological problem. It is also easy, as we said earlier, to portray Nestorius and Cyril as incarnations of good and evil (or evil and good) respectively, and thereby do them both a grave injustice. There is no doubt that both were striving for the same theological end: to avoid the unacceptable extremes of confusion of natures and separation of natures, and to make it incontrovertibly clear that the only tolerable doctrine was that there is in the one Christ an unconfused union of true God and true man. The problems lay in terminology—*Theotokos* v. *anthrōpotokos*, conjunction v. union—and also, it must be admitted, in Cyril's antagonism and underhanded tactics. Yet we must not forget that underneath the devious and unethical schemer there lay a brilliant and thoughtful theologian. Both his trinitarian and his Christological writings demonstrate the precision and acuity of his thinking, and his vehement attacks on Nestorius were not entirely without foundation. There is certainly no doubt that the latter was maligned, but there is equally no doubt that some of his ideas—and particularly his terminology—were indeed dubious. On the other hand, he did *not* say that Christ was a mere man, and there is a world of difference between using words which are unwise and making statements which are wrong. Cyril's theology was perhaps superior to his morals; Nestorius' morals were perhaps superior to his theology.

VENERATION OF THE VIRGIN. Mosaic, before 1148.

THEOTOKOS. The 'bearer of God', adapted from a sixth-century ivory panel.

CHAPTER X

THE COUNCIL OF CHALCEDON

THE UNEASY PEACE of 433 came to an end in 448. By this time Cyril of Alexandria had been dead for some four years, and John of Antioch had been dead for seven. Nestorius had been banished to the Egyptian equivalent of Siberia; Theodosius II was still nominally emperor, but was now being dominated by the Grand Chamberlain of the imperial court, the eunuch Chrysaphius; the bishop of Constantinople was Flavian, a well-meaning but weak man; and in Rome, the papacy had passed from Sixtus III, who had made some important contributions in achieving the truce of 433, to Leo the Great, that forceful, energetic, and charismatic figure who was so important for the development of papal power in the fifth century.

Chrysaphius' godfather was Eutyches, who was archimandrite—or, in western terms, abbot—of one of the major monasteries in Constantinople. By this time he was probably about seventy, and whether from senility or some other cause, his thinking was fuddled and his theology poor. He was wholly anti-Nestorius and wholly pro-Cyril, but in his support of the Cyrilline cause, he went further than ever Cyril did, and fell headlong into the pit that yawns at the outer edge of Alexandrian Christology: he confused the natures in Christ. Just how he confused them, and to what extent, is not entirely clear. Eutyches himself may not have known, for as we have said, his theological thinking left much to be desired. He certainly maintained that although there were two natures before the incarnation, there was only one nature after it (which is dangerous talk), and he certainly envisaged Christ's humanity as being somehow swallowed up or absorbed by the divinity. This, of course, is to deny that Christ was consubstantial with us, and it imperils the Christian doctrine of redemption. In other words, whatever precisely Eutyches was saying, there is no doubt that it was wrong: he *did* confuse the natures and his views were unquestionably heretical.

It was late in 448 that the matter came to a head. Eutyches, his godson Chrysaphius, and Dioscorus, Cyril's successor as patriarch of Alexandria (who, like Eutyches, was an extremist in the Cyrilline party and who considered Constantinople to be far too big for its boots), determined to put an end to the truce of 433; and Eutyches, who was an important and highly respected figure in Constantinople (despite his theological inadequacies), began openly to condemn those who maintained that after the union of Godhead and manhood in the incarnation, there still remained two natures. Almost immediately he was accused of confusing the natures (which was true), and of resurrecting the heresy of Apollinaris (which was partly true), and the case came before Flavian, the bishop of the imperial city, in November of 449.

Flavian realized immediately that Eutyches' views were unacceptable, and he had no hesitation in saying so. He, rightly, condemned and deposed him. But Eutyches appealed the sentence and wrote, defending himself, to a number of important bishops, including his friend Dioscorus of Alexandria (who he knew would support him) and the powerful Leo in Rome (who he hoped would support him). Dioscorus, of course, rallied round straightaway, and with their tremendous influence at court, he,

Eutyches, and Chrysaphius persuaded the emperor to review the case at a council to be held at Ephesus in August of 449. Leo, meanwhile, had read the minutes of Eutyches' trial (sent to him a little while earlier by Flavian) and had realized at once that Eutyches' views could not possibly be countenanced and that Flavian had been perfectly correct in deposing him. He therefore prepared a statement of the case—the so-called *Tome of Leo*—and sent it off to Flavian, assuming that it would be read at the council of Ephesus in 449.

It was not. That iniquitous council was interested neither in Leo, his legates, nor his *Tome*; nor was it much interested in theology, nor in ascertaining the true facts of the matter. It was dominated by Dioscorus, and there was never the slightest doubt about its outcome: Eutyches was reinstated, and Flavian was condemned and deposed.

Leo, bishop of what Nicaea had designated the foremost see of Christendom, was naturally incensed. He referred to the council as a 'den of thieves' and prepared for battle. Dioscorus' triumph and Eutyches' glee were short-lived, however, for in the year 450, Chrysaphius was ousted by Pulcheria (we met her in the last chapter: she was Theodosius II's elder sister), and Theodosius himself fell off his horse, sustained major injuries, and died on 28 July. Things now moved very rapidly: Pulcheria married Marcian, an intelligent soldier who then became the new emperor, Leo allied himself with Pulcheria, Chrysaphius was executed, and Dioscorus, presumably, trembled in his episcopal sandals. Then, to resolve the chaotic situation and provide a solution to these involved and violent controversies, Marcian summoned a council to meet in Chalcedon in October 451.

This was the great Council of Chalcedon, the Fourth Ecumenical Council, and the largest which the church had hitherto seen. More than five hundred bishops attended, all but four of whom were easterners, and since the real ruler of the council was Pulcheria, the results were predictable: the decisions of the council of 449—Leo's 'den of thieves'—were annulled; Dioscorus was deposed (and died in exile three years later); Flavian was reinstated; Eutyches was banished; Nestorius was re-condemned (it made little difference to him: his life was almost over); and Cyril of Alexandria and Leo of Rome were treated as inspired spokesmen of orthodoxy. The Council then drew up a statement of its own views, stipulating who was right and who was wrong, and enunciating, as clearly as possible, what it considered to be the true, official, orthodox doctrine of the universal church with regard to the person of Christ. This important document is known as *The Chalcedonian Definition of the Faith*, and we must now examine it in a little more detail.

In essence, it makes five points, as follows:

Point 1: It sets out and agrees with the 'Creed of the Three Hundred and Eighteen Holy Fathers.' This is the Creed which was introduced at the Council of Nicaea in 325, and which we translated and discussed in Chapter V.

Point 2: 'Because of those who fight against the Holy Spirit,' it sets out and agrees with the creed of the 'One Hundred and Fifty Holy Fathers who assembled in the imperial city.' 'Those who fight against the Holy Spirit' were the Pneumatomachians whom we discussed in Chapter VI, and the 'One Hundred and Fifty Holy Fathers who assembled in the imperial city' refers to the Second Ecumenical Council, the Council of Constantinople, which met in 381. Just what this creed is, however, what it says, and how it is connected with the Council of 381, are matters we shall leave aside for the moment.

Point 3: It agrees with the 'synodical letters of the blessed Cyril, shepherd of the church of Alexandria' because they refute the follies of Nestorius. These are the two great Synodical Epistles which Cyril wrote to Nestorius in the year 430, and to which we referred in Chapter IX. When they drafted this point, the fathers at Chalcedon may actually have been thinking only of the second letter, but it was not long before the third, which represents a noticeably more extreme Cyrilline position, was also understood to be included.

Point 4: It agrees with the 'Letter of the leader of the great and older Rome (Constantinople, remember, was the 'New' Rome), the most blessed and most holy archbishop Leo' because it refutes the perverse ideas of Eutyches. This is the *Tome of Leo* which we mentioned above, in which Leo, in clear and precise Latin, shows just why Eutyches was wrong and demonstrates that Christianity *must* accept a doctrine in which 'the properties of each nature and substance were preserved, and came together into one person. . . . Therefore, in the complete and perfect nature of true man there was born true God: complete in what belonged to him, complete in what belonged to us.'[1] In other words, the doctrine of unconfused union, which is now so familiar to us.

Point 5: Finally, after disposing of Nestorianism and Eutychianism, the fathers at Chalcedon set out as clearly and as concisely as possible what they considered to be the official position of the universal church on the Christological problem. Some of the language came from Cyril's second Synodical Letter; some was taken from Leo's *Tome* (and, of course, translated into Greek); a little of it derives from statements of bishop Flavian; and a considerable amount was borrowed from the *Formula of Reunion* which we discussed and, in part, translated in the last chapter. What they said was this:

Therefore, following the holy fathers, we all unanimously teach that we should confess that our Lord Jesus Christ is one and the same Son, the same perfect in his divinity, the same perfect in his humanity, truly God and truly man, the same of a rational soul and

---

[1] Leo I, *Epistola (28) Dogmatica ad Flavianum* 3.

body, consubstantial (*homoousios*) with the Father in
his divinity and the same consubstantial (*homoousios*)
with us in his humanity, like us in all things except for
sin; before the ages begotten from the Father in his
divinity, and in the last days, the same, for us and for
our salvation, [begotten] from Mary the Virgin, the
Theotokos, in his humanity; one and the same Christ,
Son, Lord, only-begotten; made known in two natures without confusion, without change, without division, without separation; the difference of the
natures being in no way removed because of the
union, but rather the specific property of each of the
two natures being preserved, and coming together in
one person and one subsistence, not parted or divided
into two persons, but one and the same Son and only-
begotten God the Word, Lord Jesus Christ.

To western eyes this was—and is—an unambiguous and
clear-cut statement. It is as precise a description as we
could hope for of the doctrine of unconfused union, and if
we read it in context, with the whole document of which it
forms the concluding part, it is quite impossible to retain
any doubts about the blasphemous unacceptability of
Nestorian separation or the iniquitous folly of Eutychian
confusion. There is one person of the incarnate Christ, and
in that one person are the two united natures of true God
and true man. There is no confusion; there is no change;
there is no division; there is no separation. Nothing could
be more precise, and the west accepted the Chalcedonian
definition and remained true to it from the time of Leo the
Great onwards.

In the east, unfortunately, this was not the case, but
before noting the reasons for this, we must return for
a moment to the second point made by the bishops at
Chalcedon and say a few words about the creed of the '150
Holy Fathers.' This creed is by far the most important and
most widely used among Christians of all varieties, both

eastern and western. It is often referred to (incorrectly) as 'the Nicene Creed,' but this is an unfortunate appellation, since it confuses it with the original creed of Nicaea which we examined in Chapter V. On other occasions it appears as 'the Nicene-Constantinopolitan Creed' or just 'the Constantinopolitan Creed', a title which intimates the traditional story of its origin. According to this tradition, what we have here is the original Creed of Nicaea with additions and elaborations added by the bishops at the Council of Constantinople in 381, additions and elaborations which were intended to refute certain heresies which had arisen since 325 and which were accordingly not dealt with in the original version. It is now well known that this tradition is incorrect, but precisely what did happen is still quite obscure. The most reasonable explanation seems to be that the creed originally derived from the Jerusalem church—though this is not certain—and that it was received in a form very similar to that which it has at present. But it also seems probable—though again not certain—that the hundred and fifty fathers at Constantinople did make certain amendments to it—how many is unknown—and that they did have a certain input into its final recension. Whatever the true story, one thing is clear: very little notice was taken of the creed between 381 and 451, and its present fame and widespread usage dates from what we might call its 'canonization' by the fathers who met at Chalcedon. Here is a literal translation:

> We believe in one God, Father, almighty, maker of heaven and earth, and of all things visible and invisible; and in one Lord Jesus Christ, the only-begotten Son of God, begotten from the Father before all ages, light from light, true God from true God, begotten not made, consubstantial (*homoousios*) with the Father, through whom all things came into being; who, because of us humans and because of our salvation, came down from the heavens and became incarnate

from the Holy Spirit and Mary the Virgin and became human, and was crucified for us under Pontius Pilate, and suffered and was buried, and rose on the third day according to the Scriptures, and ascended into the heavens, and sits on the right hand of the Father, and will come again with glory to judge the living and the dead, of whose kingdom there will be no end; and in the Holy Spirit, the lord and life-giver, who proceeds from the Father, who with Father and Son is together worshipped and together glorified, who spoke through the prophets; in one holy universal and apostolic church. We confess one baptism to the remission of sins; we look forward to a resurrection of the dead and a life of the world to come. Amen.

A careful comparison of this creed with the original creed of Nicaea (which you will find translated on pages 60–61) reveals a number of minor differences and two major ones: (1) the whole of the last paragraph dealing with the Holy Spirit, and (2) the important addition 'of whose kingdom there will be no end.' To appreciate these additions we must remember that although this creed was 'canonized' at Chalcedon, it actually dates from the late fourth century, and the section on the Holy Spirit reflects the efforts of the Cappadocian Fathers—Basil and the two Gregories—to complete the work of Athanasius and persuade people to accept a Trinity in which all three persons were consubstantial, and not just the Father and the Son. But notice the cautious way in which the passage is phrased: the Holy Spirit is described in biblical terms ('lord' comes from 2 Cor 3:17, and 'life-giver' from Rom 8:2), and it is simply said to be 'co-worshipped and co-glorified' with Father and Son. This unquestionably *implies* the full divinity of the Holy Spirit, but it does not state it, and nowhere in this final paragraph is the Holy Spirit actually referred to as 'God' or stated unequivocally to be *homoousios* with the other two persons of the Trinity. By 451 this cautious Basilean language would not have been nearly so necessary, but the Chalcedonian fathers were not prepared to devise a new creed and were unwilling to tamper with those already in existence. They preferred to remain true to the tradition they had received (or thought they had received) from their predecessors, and therefore stated that the section of the 'Constantinopolitan' Creed which dealt with the question of the substance/*ousia* of the Holy Spirit, simply clarified the very brief statement with which the original Creed of Nicaea concluded. They stressed, however, that it was clarification, not addition, for there was nothing lacking in the original Nicene Creed: it was simply in need of a certain amount of refinement.

The other passage we mentioned earlier—'of whose kingdom there will be no end'—also derives from a fourth-century milieu. Marcellus was bishop of Ancyra (the modern Ankara), and despite the fact that he did not die until about 374, his views on the Trinity echoed the ideas of an earlier century. In some ways he was similar to Hippolytus and Tertullian, who were more or less on the right side of orthodoxy, and in some ways he was similar to Praxeas, who most certainly was not. According to Marcellus, in the beginning there was just the Divine Oneness, One Alone, and only for the purposes of creation and redemption did the Divine Oneness become a Divine Threeness. Only for creation and redemption are Christ the *Logos* and the Holy Spirit put forth as separate entities, and when the work of redemption has finally been completed, they will be reabsorbed back into the Divine Oneness. Marcellus could cite St Paul to support his case—'then comes the end, when he (= Christ) delivers the kingdom to the God and Father' (1 Cor. 15:24)—but this was emphatically not the view of the Christian church. As we have seen earlier, Christianity maintains that God was *always* three and one, and to assert that there was once a time and will be a time when he will be One Alone is to imply that Christianity differs from Judaism only for a limited period. The 'Constantinopolitan' Creed therefore corrects the unacceptable views of Marcellus: since there is no end to Christ, neither is there any end to his kingdom.

Only one final point remains to be considered: the original version of the 'Constantinopolitan' Creed states quite clearly that the Holy Spirit 'proceeds from the Father.' Notice that it does not say that the Spirit proceeds 'from the Father and the Son'. Whereas the eastern churches maintained and still maintain the original wording, the western churches have amended the text to include the additional words: three of them—'and the Son'—if we are thinking in English; only one—*filioque*—if we are thinking in Latin. Why? The answer is simple: because of Augustine. As we saw at the end of Chapter VII, Augustine's great contribution to the doctrine of the Holy Spirit was to replace the idea of Single Procession ('from the Father *through* the Son') with that of Double Procession ('from the Father *and* the Son'), and his idea became the accepted teaching of the western church. For more than a century Latin Christians retained the original wording of the Creed, but then, in the late sixth century, we find the additional 'and the Son' appearing first of all in Spain, and then, slowly but insidiously, it spread throughout the whole of Europe until, by the eleventh century, it was accepted at Rome and universally in the Latin west. The east always objected to it, maintaining that creeds promulgated by ecumenical councils cannot be changed except by the authority of ecumenical councils and that the doctrine was theologically suspect because it destroyed the balance of the Trinity. But the details of the eastern objections to this brief addition, and the story of how it came to play a major role in the eventual schism of the eastern and western churches in 1054, are not matters we shall deal with in this present study.

For the west, then, Chalcedon effectively ended the Christological dispute. The *Chalcedonian Definition* did not explain *how* the divinity and humanity were united in the one person of Jesus of Nazareth (something wholly inexplicable), but it did state that they *were* united, and that they were united without confusion, change, division, or separation. The situation in the east, however, was much more complex and much more violent, and we must now direct both our time and our attention to an investigation of the problems which occurred.

PANTOCRATOR. Christ the creator and judge, adapted from a ninth-century byzantime mosaic ceiling.

CHAPTER XI

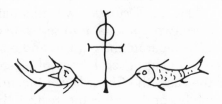

CHRIST AFTER CHALCEDON

AD THE COUNCIL OF CHALCEDON been conducted in
Latin and its *Definition* penned in Latin for a Latin-
speaking world, the savagery, bigotry, bitterness,
and murder which ravaged the eastern church after the
Council might have been somewhat reduced. It would not
have been reduced to nothing, for the theological problems
were often simply masks for political and nationalistic
problems, but it might certainly have been ameliorated. If
we say, in Latin, that Christ was one person (*persona*) in
whom were united two natures (*naturae*) or substances
(*substantiae*), then the statement is unambiguous. 'Substance' does not and can not mean 'person' in Latin, and
we cannot therefore be saying either that Christ was one
nature or that he was two persons. In Greek, unfortunately, this was not the case. The word which was used
in the *Chalcedonian Definition* for 'nature' was *physis* (we can
see it in the English word 'physics,' the study of the *natural*
properties of matter and energy, or 'physiology,' the study
of the processes of *natural* life), and *physis* could mean not
only 'nature' (which was what the Chalcedonian fathers
intended it to mean), but also 'individual creature' or 'independent entity' or 'person.' For those who understood

the term in this way, therefore, the statement in the *Definition* that Christ was 'made known in two natures' (*physeis*:
the Greek plural of the word) was out-and-out heresy.
According to them, the *Definition* was maintaining that in
Christ there were two persons, two separate entities, and
to say that was to separate the natures and resurrect, in all
its wickedness, the supposed heresy of Nestorius. If this
were indeed the case, the *Chalcedonian Definition* was stat-
ing quite formally, and asking the rest of the church to
accept, that Christ was no more than an inspired man.

Those people who read nature (*physis*) as *person*, therefore, correctly maintained that Christ was not two natures,
but one, and they could defend their view by citing Cyril of
Alexandria who, it will be remembered, was treated in the
Chalcedonian Definition as an infallible voice of orthodox
doctrine. Did not Cyril say that in Christ there was *'one*
nature (*physis*) of the Word of God enfleshed'? Indeed he
did, and by 'nature' he meant the one single, independent
person of Jesus of Nazareth. But the extent to which the
issue had become confused is clearly apparent when we
consider the source of Cyril's famous phrase. Cyril himself
believed it came from the great Athanasius, but if you turn
back in this book to page 95, you will find, unfortunately,
that it actually derives from the heretic and blasphemer
Apollinaris.

The situation has obviously become ridiculous. For
Apollinaris, 'nature' is 'nature,' but for Cyril, quoting
Apollinaris (without realising his source), 'nature' is 'person.' For those who supported Chalcedon, 'nature' is 'nature.' For Leo and the west, it is *'natura,'* and was never
anything else. For those who opposed Chalcedon and
thought they were supporting Cyril, 'nature' is 'person.'
And so on.

Added to this, there were still plenty of people around
who had supported the influential Eutyches and still supported him, despite the decisions at Chalcedon, and there
still remained considerable numbers of Nestorians who

still thought Nestorius had been unjustly condemned. The Eutychians, therefore, absolutely refused to acknowledge two natures in Christ, and the Nestorians absolutely refused to acknowledge one. Nor was the conflict limited simply to verbal warfare. Consider the case of Proterius. After Eutyches' friend, Dioscorus, had been deposed and banished by the Council of Chalcedon, Proterius was appointed in his place as bishop of Alexandria. As a Chalcedonian appointment he naturally supported the *Chalcedonian Definition*, but when he returned to Alexandria he found his Christian flock totally opposed both to it and to him. Alexandria was passionately Cyrilline, and if Cyril had said 'one nature,' then 'one nature' it was. So great was the antagonism that Proterius found that he could maintain his position only with military support, but in 457, when the Alexandrians rioted following the death of the emperor Marcian, this proved futile. Set upon by the mob, he was beaten to death, and his body burned in the local stadium.

In the east, therefore, far from settling the Christological problem, Chalcedon had generated a further division. On the one hand were the Chalcedonians—those who supported the council and agreed with its *Definition*—who, like Leo and the west, were perfectly happy to acknowledge Christ in two natures (where *physis* = nature); and on the other was that large group, located primarily in Egypt and Syria, who refused to do so and, following Cyril, would speak only of one nature (where *physis* = person). This latter group therefore became known as the Monophysites or 'One-nature-ites' and the Chalcedonians as the Dyophysites or 'Two-nature-ites.' But as we said earlier, the terminological differences only concealed much greater nationalistic and political antagonisms. To the Egyptians and Syrians, the Council of Chalcedon appeared as an attempt to impose a foreign—i.e., Greek-Constantinopolitan—imperial domination, for it must be remembered that at this time both the Egyptians and the Syrians had native cultures quite distinct from that of the rest of the Graeco-Roman world. Much of the populace did not even speak Greek—the Syrians spoke Syriac and the Egyptians spoke Coptic—and in any case, Alexandria and Constantinople had existed for decades in a state of mutual hostility. 'Chalcedonian' and 'Monophysite' thus became nationalistic and political slogans, and there were probably comparatively few who really understood—or who were much interested in understanding—the subtle theological arguments which lay behind them. To suggest that the conflict could have been resolved theologically would be like saying that the ghastly situation in Northern Ireland could be remedied simply by persuading each side to admit that the other was Christian (although on second thought, that in itself would be no mean accomplishment).

Nevertheless, an attempt was made, and since it established a precarious peace for about forty years, it deserves some consideration. In 482, twenty-five years after Marcian had died and Proterius had been lynched, the emperor was Zeno and the patriarch of Constantinople was Acacius. The patriarch, with the assistance of the bishop of Alexandria and the support and sponsorship of the emperor, drew up a compromise proposal called the *Henoticon*, a Greek word which means 'The Unifier' or 'The Uniter.' In this document we find, firstly, an acceptance of both the Creed of Nicaea and the 'Constantinopolitan Creed' and, secondly, a condemnation of both Nestorius and Eutyches. So far all is in accordance with the *Chalcedonian Definition*. But then, to conciliate the Cyrilline Monophysites, we have, thirdly, an acceptance of Cyril's Twelve Anathemas (these were a series of short anti-Nestorian definitions which were appended to his Third Synodical Letter and which represent the more extreme form of his teaching), and, fourthly, to conciliate everybody, the statement that Christ is consubstantial with the Father in his divinity and with us in our humanity (which was stated in the *Chalcedonian Definition*), that he was incarnate from the Holy Spirit and the Virgin Mary *Theotokos* (so too the *Chalcedonian Definition*), and that he is *one*, not *two*. In precisely what he is 'one, not two' is not defined, and people could fill in the blanks for themselves. To an Alexandrian Monophysite, he is one (nature); to a Chalcedonian Dyophysite, he is one (person). But no one could deny that Christ was one something, not two somethings, and that was precisely Acacius's point. Fifthly and finally, the *Henoticon* anathematized anyone who held or who holds an opinion different from this, 'whether put forward at Chalcedon or at any other council,' a statement which acknowledged that Chalcedon *might* have been wrong (as the Monophysites maintained), but might also have been right (the view of the Chalcedonians).

In the east this artful document produced a general, if not universal, agreement, and from 482 to about 520 it was accepted as the standard of orthodoxy. But in the west, the reaction was very different. Rome objected to the *Henoticon* partly because it conceded that the fathers at Chalcedon *could* have been misguided (and Rome had accepted the *Chalcedonian Definition* almost from the start), and partly because bishop Acacius had promulgated the *Henoticon* without consulting the pope. Added to this was the further complication that Rome, rather than supporting the bishop who was then occupying the see of Alexandria, was putting all of its considerable weight behind a rival claimant. The consequences were inevitable: Pope Felix III, a stubborn and authoritarian prelate with a violent temper, was predictably incensed, and in his fury he excommunicated the patriarch of Constantinople in July 484. The sentence of excommunication was sent to the imperial city by special messenger, and eventually pinned to Acacius's vestments by some over-enthusiastic monks while he was in church celebrating the Divine Liturgy. Acacius' response was simply to remove the name of the pope from the diptychs. Why? Because the diptychs were lists of Christians, living and dead, for whom special prayers were offered at the

Eucharist, and to exclude a particular name from the list was to imply that the person concerned was not orthodox. It also implied, by extension, that he had been excommunicated. This was the beginning of the 'Acacian Schism', the first schism between the eastern and western churches, which lasted from 484 to the accession to the throne of the emperor Justin I in 518.

Even in the east, however, the *Henoticon* failed to achieve a lasting peace. It is all very well to say 'one, not two,' but there comes a time when further avoidance of the problem is intolerable, and you feel the need to grab your episcopal neighbour by his purple stock, or whatever, hold him up against the wall, and ask 'one *WHAT*'? So despite the appearance in the east of a number of brilliant and sometimes conciliatory theologians during the forty years or so when the *Henoticon* was accepted, the situation gradually deteriorated, and by about 515 the two sides were once again in active opposition.

Other attempts at reconciliation during the sixth century were even less successful than the *Henoticon*. In fact, they succeeded not at all. But in the following century, a further effort was made which did seem, at first, to be much more effective, but which led to the curious situation of a doctrine of the person of Christ which was patently heretical being approved by the emperor and many of his bishops as the official teaching of church and state.

As was so often the case, the circumstances which led to this situation were political rather than theological. The eastern emperor, Heraclius, was deeply concerned about increasing attacks on the empire by the Persians and, later on, by the Arabs, and it would obviously be much to his advantage to reconcile the internal divisions within his realm and face the external aggressors with a united people. He therefore consulted with the Monophysite leaders in 624 and they came up with the suggestion that although it could be admitted that in Christ there were indeed two natures, there was only one 'energy' or 'operation' or 'activity' (the Greek word can mean all three things). By this they meant that it was one and the same Son who was the subject of every activity or operation, and that we must never separate the natures by suggesting that one particular activity pertained to the human son of Mary while another pertained only to the divine Son of God. No longer, therefore, do we speak of 'two natures before the incarnation and one nature after it,' or 'two natures in one person.' We now say 'two natures, but one mode of activity.'

Heraclius sent the proposal off to Sergius, the patriarch of Constantinople, who gladly accepted it, and once it was promulgated the results, at least in part, were just what Heraclius had hoped: the Monophysites liked it, and flocked back into the orthodox fold. Unfortunately, the hard-line Chalcedonians utterly rejected it, and as a consequence of this rejection, Sergius decided to write to the pope (a good Chalcedonian, as were they all) and seek his opinion. The pope at the time was Honorius, an able manager and excellent administrator, but between repairing the Roman aqueducts and managing the papal finances he seems to have had little time to spare for the intricacies of theology. His reply to Sergius, therefore, was both hasty and unfortunate, for not only did he give his approval to the new idea, but went on to say that since it was God the *Logos* who operated or acted through both natures, this was effectively the equivalent of saying that in Christ there was only one will.

This was more than Heraclius and Sergius had ever hoped for. They seized on the phrase 'one will' with wild cries of delight, and in 638 Heraclius issued the *Ekthesis* ('The Edict' or 'The Explanation') which stated the official imperial view of the matter: there shall in future be no more mention of 'energies' or 'operations' or 'activities,' whether one or two, and all Christians shall confess (whether they like it or not) that there are in Christ two natures united in a single will. Because the Greek word for one alone is *monos* and the word for will is *thelēma*, this doctrine came to be known as Mono-thelet-ism, 'One-will-ism.'

That this doctrine is wrong there can be no doubt. That is to say, from a Christian standpoint monothelitism cannot be reconciled with the Christian tradition. To maintain that there is only one will in Christ is, effectively, to deny the real existence and activity of the human will; and to deny a human will in Christ is, in essence, to resurrect the old heresy of Apollinaris, which had been unmasked and condemned two and a half centuries earlier by the Cappadocian Fathers. How, then, could Honorius have been so stupid as to suggest it?

Honorius' problem was not stupidity, but speed. He failed to take the care he needed to take, and there is no doubt that he did *not* mean 'one will' in the sense in which the term appears in the *Ekthesis*. What he meant was that whereas there are *two* wills in Christ—divine and human—there could never be any real conflict between them, for if any conflict did arise, the divine will would ultimately prevail. Furthermore, if you have two wills acting in complete harmony and unison, is this really distinguishable from one single will? No, thought Honorius, it is not, and we cannot deny that he has a point. So what he was really saying, but saying very badly, was that although *psychologically* there are two wills in Christ, *functionally* they act in agreement as one.

Honorius died in October of 638 just before the *Ekthesis* was issued, but his successors saw immediately that Monotheletism was theologically intolerable and, to the great annoyance of the eastern emperor (who saw it as being politically essential), had no hesitation in condemning it. This opposition came to a head with the Lateran Council of 649 and the remarkable and tragic events surrounding the life and death of Pope Martin I.

By this time Heraclius was dead and had been succeeded by Constans II. The new emperor realized that the *Ekthesis* was causing problems, so he withdrew it and substituted for it another edict called the *Typos* ('The Model' or 'The Plan'). But all this document said was that in future no one should speak either of one will or of two wills, and that the matter was not a subject for further discussion. This, of course, was absurd, since human beings have never, at any time, been able to keep their mouths shut, and the surest way of persuading anyone to do anything at all is to forbid them to do it. Pope Martin, a most courageous man, took the bull by the horns, anathematized Monotheletism, and at the same time condemned outright the imperial *Typos*.

Constans, naturally, was infuriated, and immediately ordered the pope to be arrested and brought to Constantinople. He sent one of his chamberlains to do the job, and in a remarkable series of incidents the latter tracked down the pope to the Lateran basilica (where he was ill in bed), deposed him, arrested him, smuggled him out of Rome, and brought him to the imperial capital on 17th September 653. There he was tried, found guilty, flogged, and condemned to death (he already had dysentery and severe gout), but at the request of the patriarch of Constantinople, the death sentence was commuted to banishment. Not that it made any difference: he was kept in prison for a further three months in revolting conditions and then taken to the Crimea where, on 16 September 655, he soon died from starvation, the climate, and plain brutality. He was the last of the martyr-popes.

Monotheletism lingered on for a further twenty-five years. The west, as we have seen, never accepted it, and eastern theologians, too, were well aware of its dangers. Its most formidable opponent was Maximus, a learned and holy man who, after holding the post of Imperial Secretary under Heraclius, entered the monastic life in about 614. Maximus, like Martin, realized the inadequacy of Monotheletism, and realized too that the Chalcedonians and the

Monophysites were both, at heart, trying to say the same thing: that in Jesus of Nazareth we see an unconfused union of divinity and humanity in one incarnate Lord. But his efforts to make these matters clear earned imperial disapproval, and Maximus, like Martin, was arrested. Because his tongue had continued to speak of two wills, despite imperial orders, Constans had it torn out; and because his right hand had refused to sign certain compromising documents, Constans had it cut off. Maximus, too, was exiled, and again like Martin, died soon afterwards on the 13 August 662.

The work of Maximus, Martin, and their colleagues found its fulfilment at the Council of Constantinople in 680 (the Sixth Ecumenical Council, held after the death of Constans), which stated unequivocally (1) that in Christ there are two natures; (2) that as a consequence of this there are two wills and two activities; but (3) that there is nevertheless a complete harmony between the divine and human wills, and likewise between the divine and human activities. With the decrees of this council, Monotheletism ceased to be a problem. It had existed for more than fifty years when it should never, really, have existed at all; but since it was primarily a political, rather than a theological heresy, the theological arguments were frequently secondary to the political realities.

Monophysitism, on the other hand, never came to an end at all. None of the attempts at reconciliation ever succeeded in achieving any permanent resolution, and although the major part of the Christian world accepted the Chalcedonian statement, three great churches, from the sixth century until the present, have refused to do so: the Coptic Orthodox Church in Egypt, the Syrian Jacobites, and the Armenian Orthodox Church. They are still, in terminology, Monophysite, and although most—perhaps all—of their theologians now recognize that there is no essential difference between the Monophysite and Dyophysite understandings of the person of Christ, they have naturally, over a period of fourteen centuries, developed their own very distinctive organizations. At a meeting in 1964 representatives of monophysite and dyophysite orthodox churches stated officially that they acknowledged in each other the one orthodox faith; that they found themselves in total agreement on the essential Christological dogmas; and that they recognized that the same truth was being expressed in different terminologies. From the murder of Proterius to the martyrdom of Martin this, regrettably, was not the case; but whenever theology is transformed into politics, morality and truth take second place to political necessity, and when reason gives way to the rule of the mob, then all of us are doomed.

AUGUSTINE OF HIPPO. Adapted from a sixth-century fresco.

CHAPTER XII

A QUESTION OF GRACE

W E HAVE NOW AGREED that Christ the *Logos* is truly God and consubstantial with the Father and the Holy Spirit; and we have also agreed that this divine Word became incarnate in the one unconfused person of Jesus of Nazareth, who was perfect God and perfect man. We have also noted, in both the Creed of Nicaea and the Creed of 'Constantinople,' that the reason for this incarnation was 'because of us humans and because of our salvation.' How, then, does salvation work? In what way are we to be saved? According to the writer of the letter to the Ephesians, the answer is simple and straightforward: 'You have been saved by grace' (Eph 2:6). But what is grace, and how does it work, and how are we to reconcile it with the idea of free will? Is grace essential, or merely useful? Does everyone need it, or only some? And if I work really hard, live a life of the utmost piety, keep all the commandments, exhibit true charity, and feed all the stray cats in the neighbourhood, can I be saved without it? To answer these questions we must visit the Garden of Eden and see what happened there.

141

First of all, both east and west were agreed that in Eden Adam and Eve were in a state of blessedness, perfection, and complete happiness. They were immortal; they could talk freely with God; all their wants, both of body and soul, were fully satisfied. The view of the easterners was somewhat more metaphysical than that of the westerners (Gregory of Nazianzus, for example, visualized the Garden of Eden as the world of the Platonic Ideas), but both were agreed on the essential point.

All Christians also agreed that Adam and Eve fell. They ate the forbidden fruit and thereby inherited mortality, a susceptibility to corruption and disease, and a tendency to sin. Again, the west laid greater stress than did the east on this last point, but again, both were agreed on the essentials.

Thirdly, all agreed that the consequences of this sin were not restricted to Adam and Eve, but were in some way passed down to their descendants, i.e., to us. The process by which this transmission occurred was not quite clear, but that it did occur was not in doubt. One theory held that the soul of a child was generated in some mysterious way from the souls of its parents, much as its body was formed from their bodies; and since the souls of Adam and Eve were tainted, the souls they generated were also naturally tainted, and these tainted souls produced, in turn, further tainted souls, all the way down to us. According to this theory, which was called *Traducianism* (the Latin verb *traduco* means 'to bring over,' and the soul of the infant is 'brought over' from the souls of its parents), sin is transmitted like a congenital disease; but although it makes the transmission of sin easy to understand, this theory was to be condemned by the church, partly because it is difficult to reconcile with the wholly spiritual nature of the soul, and partly because, by suggesting that the souls of children might in some way be produced or generated by the souls of their parents, it imperils the idea of God as the only creator. Instead, the church approved *Creationism*, the doctrine that each soul is created anew by God at the moment individual existence begins, and although this view accounts splendidly for the spirituality of the soul, it makes it much more difficult to explain just how a brand-new creation, straight from the hands of God, could possibly be corrupted by someone else's sin. Yet corrupted it was—of that the fathers were not in doubt—and the only way they could explain it was by proposing a 'spiritual' or 'mystical' unity of later humanity with its first parents. Again, there was a difference of emphasis: the west laid greater stress on this mystical unity than did the east, but neither denied its reality. As a consequence of this inherited taint, our natural inclination is to sin, and we need only glance around this chaotic world in which we live to see this inclination in action.

The eastern fathers never denied the existence of free will and never denied the human ability to do good, even though doing it was difficult. On the other hand, they were also agreed that of one's own power one could not do enough good to achieve salvation. For this we need grace, the supernatural assistance of God. But because we can do *some* good, it is incumbent upon us to do it, and thereby 'deserve' or 'earn' or 'merit' God's further help. By his grace we were given free will in the beginning, and by his grace we may use that will to do good and thus become deserving of grace in yet greater abundance. It is like the parable of the prodigal son: the young man who had spent all his money had to make the first move: he had to get up and leave the pigs, and then, while he was still a long way off, his father saw him and came running to meet him. That, for the east, was (and is) how grace operates.

This was also the view of the western fathers up to the time of Augustine. They laid greater stress than did the east on the difficulty of making the first move, but they were, on the whole, convinced that if you do not stir yourself, then you will get nowhere. Neither east nor west believed that the father of the prodigal son was going to send a limousine to collect him, and neither east nor west believed that he would eventually be saved simply by sitting with the pigs and waiting for something to happen.

At this stage, in the early fifth century, Augustine of Hippo came into conflict with Pelagius, and everything changed. Pelagius was a Briton, probably a monk, who arrived in Rome in about 400 and acquired a reputation—apparently quite justified—for his piety, austerity, and learning. As a creationist, he could not accept that human beings were so corrupted at birth that they could not help sinning, and he disagreed profoundly with the principle underlying Augustine's prayer to God for control over his sexual urges: 'Give what you command and command what you will.' What Pelagius thought Augustine was saying was 'Tell me what to do and then do it for me'. This, surely, is to put the entire burden onto God, and as far as the ascetic Pelagius was concerned, it was a denial of free will and human responsibility, and an insult to the Creator. If we are not responsible for our vices or our virtues, then no just God can either blame or praise us. I cannot be blamed for arriving late for an appointment if the taxi in which I am travelling runs out of fuel.

Pelagius, then, as a creationist, takes creationism to its logical conclusion: the soul of an infant is *not* tainted by the sin of Adam, and every infant has complete freedom of choice to do good or to do evil. Does this then mean that the Fall had no effect at all? On the contrary, said Pelagius, it had a very profound effect: it set us a bad example, and it is an example we tend to follow.

Now it is very easy to underestimate Pelagius' teaching on this point. It is all very well to say that the Fall 'set us a bad example,' but why *should* we imitate it? If we have complete freedom of will, why not just say No? The reason becomes clear once we remember that human beings are socialized from their birth onwards. How children behave, and, to a large extent, think, is conditioned by the family or society in which they are brought up, and if they are brought up in a society in which it is acceptable behaviour to spit on the floor and pick one's nose in public, then that is what they will do. It follows, then, that since Adam's children were brought up in a family which had begun to sin, they, too, sinned. And so also did their children and their children's children; and that is why we, too, have just the same problem. We are 'socialized' to sin, 'conditioned' to sin—yet not doomed to sin or forced to sin by any congenital taint or spiritual deformity.

So is there any need for grace, or can we stop this incessant and imitative sinning of our own free will? Pelagius maintains clearly that there is a need for grace (he is often misunderstood on this point), and that grace operates in a number of ways: there is initially the grace of free-will itself by which we can choose freely between righteousness and wickedness; secondly, there is the grace of revelation in the Scriptures, both Old and New, by which the paths of good and evil are laid out before us; and thirdly, there is the grace of forgiveness of sins which operates in baptism and in penance and which comes into play when, like all people, we err and stray and fall short of the glory of God. Pelagius, as we have said, insists on the need for all three forms of grace. But why? If sin is simply a habit, why not give it up tomorrow? To appreciate why not, consider yourself. Find a good, solid, ingrained habit (biting your nails, smoking, fiddling with your earrings, chewing your pen, saying 'you know?' or 'right?' after every sentence, other, more private, pleasures —there is no difficulty in discovering an example), and stop it. Now. Immediately. And never do it again. *Then* you will see the immense difficulty of such a task, and realize that we are as addicted to sin as a heroin addict is to heroin. In theory, we *can* give it up; in practice, most of us need professional help—and in the case of sin, that professional help is the grace of God.

How, then, does grace work for Pelagius? Perhaps the best way to understand it is by using the analogy of a coach and competitors at an athletics event. First of all, the competitors enter the arena with a perfectly free choice of whether and when to run, walk, kick, punch, or jump. Secondly, as the coach, I can stand on the side-lines, shout encouraging comments, and tell the competitors what to do and when to do it. And thirdly, if my team makes a mistake or fails to take my advice, I can tell them that it does not really matter, that their sins are forgiven them, that in future they should listen to their coach, but that they do not have to leave the area immediately and throw themselves off the nearest cliff or hang themselves from the nearest tree. But at no time can I enter the ring or the field and add my strength and skill to theirs, and I certainly cannot rush in, open their mouths wide, climb down inside them, and compete for them.

For Pelagius, then, we are all competitors (competitors with ingrained bad habits) and Christ is the coach. Without his instructions and continual encouragement we by ourselves may not be able to triumph, and his presence is therefore essential to us to tell us what to do and how and when to do it. But this is really as far as Pelagius goes. His concept of grace is essentially a concept of 'encouraging' or 'exhortatory' grace, whereas the great majority of the other Christian Fathers of his time preferred to think in terms of 'assisting' or 'cooperating' grace (in which Christ actively cooperates with you in doing what you do), and, as we shall see, Augustine's idea was one of 'effecting' grace (in which Christ enters inside you and effects the whole matter himself). And although the idea of 'encouraging' grace is perfectly logical, there is no doubt, as Augustine realized, that it is a view which is open to serious criticism. It implies, for example, that if you are a *very* good competitor, a real natural at the sport, you may not need the coach's advice at all and may be able to win the race or game or fight by your own unaided power. It could signify, too, that the most important aspect of Christ's incarnation was its exemplary and instructive quality—a model for us to imitate—and that his agony, death, resurrection, and ascension may not have been wholly necessary or, at least, were not necessary in quite the same sense as the rest of the Christian church defined necessity.

For Augustine, this was a denial of the basic principle of Christianity. It was a degradation of grace and an insult to the Son of God and he would have nothing whatever to do with it. His own view was diametrically different: grace was not, emphatically not, something given to us simply to help us do more easily what we can naturally do of our own power. Grace is something which must be given to us if we are to do anything at all. Without it we cannot do a single good act, and without it, as a consequence, we are doomed. Let us now consider Augustine's arguments and see how he arrives at this conclusion.

Since Adam was our first parent, said Augustine, all of us existed potentially in him. We did not exist in actual, bodily form, but in potentiality, since there was no other source from which we could have come save from the loins of Adam. Therefore, since we all existed potentially in Adam, where Adam went, we went, and what Adam did, we did. And since Adam sinned, so we all sinned in Adam, and St Paul says so: 'Through one man sin entered this world, and through sin, death, and thus death passed on to all people, for in him all sinned' (Rom 5:12). To be more precise, this is Augustine's reading of the Latin translation of this verse from Romans: the original Greek simply says '. . . and thus death passed on to all people *because* all sinned'; but the incorrect Latin translation does not in any way affect Augustine's logic.

Since we all fell 'in Adam,' so we are what Adam was in consequence: fallen, damned, doomed, condemned. At birth we are simply 'one lump of sin' and because we are so totally, so hopelessly corrupted, we can no more do good of our own power than a blind man can see or someone with no legs get up and walk. It is just impossible. Of our own power, we can only fall.

God's grace, therefore, is absolutely essential: not just useful, not just convenient, not just helpful, but *essential*. And since we are unable—not just unwilling—to do good, this grace can never be 'merited' or 'deserved.' We are no longer like the prodigal son in the parable: we *cannot* make the first move. We have been tied hand and foot, gagged, eyelids sewed shut, ears plugged, and buried up to our necks in the earth. We can do absolutely nothing unless God provides us with his grace (i.e., digs us up and cuts our bonds), and then directs our steps to heaven. Grace, therefore, is not something which helps us do better what we can already do ourselves, but something which enables us to do what is otherwise wholly outside the bounds of human possibility.

To whom, then, is this grace made available? *Answer*: to whom God wills. How many of these fortunates are there? *Answer*: God knows! But in one text Augustine says that the number of those to whom grace will be made available is the same as the number of the angels who fell with Lucifer, so that the population of the heavenly Jerusalem will remain constant. But why should I be chosen to receive this grace and not you (or vice-versa)? *Answer*: the decisions of God are inscrutable (Augustine is quoting Rom 11:33), but since God is by definition fair and just, what he does must also be fair and just, even if we cannot appreciate it. Which is no great comfort if one is on one's way to hell.

In other words, what we have here is the Augustinian doctrine of *predestination*, the doctrine which maintains that only those who are predestined to receive grace may be saved, and that all others are doomed. But what of the statement in 1 Timothy that 'God wishes *all* people to be saved' (1 Tim 2:4)? Does not this contradict the principle? No, says Augustine, it does not: what it means is 'God wants all those who are so predestined to be saved,' and that does not include everyone.

The views of Pelagius, of the eastern church in general, and of the redoubtable Augustine therefore represent the three possible ways in which human initiative may—or may not—operate. Pelagius held that we are born with a will absolutely free and totally untainted by Adam's sin; we therefore retain the possibility of saving ourselves. The easterners held that we are born with a will corrupted by Adam's sin, but not so corrupted that we cannot do at least a few good actions; in response to these actions God makes his grace available, and in cooperation with this grace, and *only* in cooperation with this grace, we can achieve salvation. Augustine held that we are born with a soul completely corrupted by Adam's sin and cannot do any good action at all; our salvation is therefore entirely in the hands of God, and if he does not make his grace available to us, there is absolutely nothing that we can do about it. Pelagian infants, we might say, are born with 20–20 vision; Greek infants are in need of spectacles; Augustinian infants are born blind.

What, then, can we say of free will? Does not the Augustinian doctrine effectively annihilate human freedom? Despite the various subtle defences of the doctrine, there is no doubt that it does. For a soul which has not yet received grace may have free will, but cannot use it freely. It is so corrupted that it can only sin. It is just as if you put me in the middle of an open field and then build a six-foot wall immediately behind me, another such wall two inches from my left hand, and another two inches from my right. Do I still have free will? Yes. Can I use it freely? No, because I can only move in one single direction. Free will therefore becomes like a eunuch's member: all show and no power.

After grace has been received, free will may perhaps play a greater role, but even then there are problems. Our will may cooperate with God's will, but only after God (who knows all things) has so arranged matters that this is bound to occur. God knows in advance what stimulus or motive will cause us to perform a particular action; he knows what action he wants to occur; and he arranges for the necessary stimulus or motive accordingly. But again, we are no more than puppets dancing to the tune of the Master Puppeteer. And it is no answer to say that our free will is most free when it is freely put into the service of the Creator, since (a) it cannot be put into his service unless he so determines; (b) it cannot be kept there unless he so arranges; and (c) if our will is entirely his will, it becomes problematical as to whether it can be called ours at all. These are undoubtedly complex matters, and there are no easy solutions, and although later Latin theologians, from the ninth century onwards, felt obliged to grapple with the problem, a consideration of these later attempts at elucidation is fortunately outside the realm of this present book.

The sombre and depressing doctrine of Augustine—sombre and depressing, that is, if one is not one of the elect—was certainly not received with favour by all parties. To condemn Pelagius was one thing (no church, either eastern or western, was prepared to deny some taint or corruption from Adam's foolishness, and no church, either eastern or western, was prepared to assert that we can be saved without grace), but to go to the other extreme and embrace Augustinian predestinationism was quite another. The situation was also exacerbated by the fact that Augustine's statements on the question tended to become more and more rigorous the more they were repeated, and even his own supporters began, in many instances, to shy away from his inexorable logic. Others were much more outspoken in their opposition: Julian, the Pelagian bishop of Eclanum (a town near Benevento in southern Italy), maintained that Augustine's pessimism (a) contradicted the principle stated in Genesis 1:25 that when God viewed his creation, he saw that it was good; (b) denied the statement in 1 Timothy 2:4 that God's will was that *all* should be saved; and (c) was a consequence of Augustine's adolescent obsession with sex—and Julian was not alone in this opinion. Even among those who, on the whole, were favourable to Augustine, attempts were made to mitigate the rigours of his doctrine. In the monasteries of southern France, for example, competent thinkers such as John Cassian or Vincent of Lérins came up with a compromise—more than a millenium later to be designated 'Semi-Pelagianism'—which was, in its essentials, much the same as the position accepted by the eastern churches: namely, that though grace was essential for salvation, humanity had not totally lost its ability for good as a consequence of Adam's sin. These ideas proved popular and were widely accepted in certain parts of France and Britain for about a century, but there was always the problem that the reputation of Augustine was growing so rapidly in the west that to criticize him was like criticizing God's private secretary, and that to oppose Augustine could easily be mistaken for supporting Pelagianism which had been condemned again and again by the church from the early fifth century onwards.

It had been condemned at Carthage and Mileve in 416, condemned by Pope Innocent I in 417, condemned again at Carthage in 418, condemned at the Council of Ephesus in 431, condemned at the second council of Orange (together with 'Semi-Pelagianism') in 529, and then gradually disappeared during the course of the sixth century. As a consequence of these councils the churches declared (1) that Adam was not created mortal, but became mortal through sin (the Pelagians maintained that Adam was mortal from the start); (2) that all persons have been contaminated in some way by Adam's fall; (3) that God's grace is not available only for the forgiveness of sins already committed, but is necessary to prevent us from committing further sins; and (4) that grace does not simply enable us to do more easily what we can already do of our own free-will—in other words, a person in whom God's grace operates is different in kind, not just in degree, from a person in whom grace is not to be found.

In the west, the Augustinian view triumphed. It is true that certain of the more rigorous aspects of his doctrine were quietly set to one side—no western theologians (until Calvin) much cared for hard-line predestinationism—but the Augustinian view of the utter corruption of human nature and the essentiality of grace came to dominate western moral theology. In the east, the situation was rather different. The Pelagian controversy had been primarily a western controversy—it had been conducted almost entirely in Latin, not Greek—and although the eastern fathers were aware of what was going on, they were, with a few exceptions, spectators rather than players. The condemnation of Pelagianism at Ephesus in 431 was a condemnation of Pelagius, not an endorsement of Augustine, and Augustine's views on the question of grace (written in Latin and addressed to Latins) were read by few easterners, and had only a very limited effect on eastern teaching. The Greek churches remained true to their more optimistic view and have remained loyal to it ever since. Yet it must be clearly understood that although the eastern and western churches differed in their assessment of innate human depravity, they were entirely in agreement that salvation could not be achieved without grace, and they were likewise in agreement that the possibility of salvation was in some way intimately linked to the incarnation of the Son of God. But what was the precise nature of this linkage, and how was it that the life and death of a single man could have such a profound effect upon the whole human race? It is to a consideration of this question and its numerous answers that we must now turn our attention.

THE FALL. Wallpainting, fourth-century.

CHRIST THE TEACHER. Adapted from a fifth-century ivory pyx.

CHAPTER XIII

CUR DEUS HOMO?

WHY DID GOD BECOME HUMAN?', *Cur Deus Homo*, is the title of a justly famous treatise by an eleventh-century archbishop of Canterbury called Anselm. It is a remarkable and impressive work, and in focussing attention on the question of just how the redemption took place, it gave rise to a whole series of complex controversies in which different theologians and different schools of theology asserted and defended their own particular views. In the centuries subsequent to Anselm, therefore, we find in the west a huge mass of material on this subject, much of it carefully and systematically presented, but in the centuries with which we are here concerned this is not the case. The question was asked—of course it was—but the detail, comprehensiveness, and systematic presentation which we find in the Middle Ages is not to be found in the earlier period.

Furthermore, it is not a question which can be answered simply. To ask why God became human is to ask the reason for his birth, life, teaching, betrayal, death, resurrection, and ascension, and it may well be that no one answer will suffice. It's like asking people why they have a particular job: there may be a number of reasons—they enjoy the work, or they feel a need to get out of the house, or they like their fellow-workers, or (most important) they need the money—all of these are true, but all combine together, and at any particular time one reason may be more relevant than another. In the same way we do not find, and should not expect to find, one single theory which presents the one single answer to Anselm's question. There are instead a number of theories, and the fathers of the church will use one at one time, another at another, and some or all may appear in juxtaposition in the same treatise, on the same page, or even in the same paragraph. 'Theories,' in fact, is a bad word to use, for it implies a certain mutual exclusiveness—to hold 'theory' A suggests that you cannot hold 'theories' B and C as well— and a wiser way of looking at the question is to view the same Christ under four different aspects: Christ as Teacher, Christ as Restorer, Christ as Victor, and Christ as Victim. Any one of these four aspects may then be dominant at any one time, but one in no way excludes the others. There was, after all, only one Christ.

For the earliest writers—the Apostolic Fathers—Christ as Teacher was of paramount importance. We have been called from darkness to light, says Clement of Rome, from ignorance to the knowledge of the glory of his name. Christ has revealed to us the truth, the whole truth, the perfect law, the way to salvation, the road to immortality, the paths of faith. The eyes of the Apostolic Fathers look to heaven rather than earth, and salvation for them is something which will happen in the future, when all are judged according to their deserts, and those who have lived a life in accordance with Christ's teachings will be rewarded with eternal bliss. They *say* that Christ was crucified for us and suffered for our sakes; they *say* that for us he died and rose again. But what they say on these matters is, on the whole, fairly formal, and they offer little evidence of really having thought about what the phrases mean. For them, the way to salvation can be summarized as 'Do what

Christ told you, and you'll go to heaven'—which is also, so far as I can see, the attitude of the majority of present-day church-goers.

For the Apologists, too, Christ as Teacher was of great importance. This becomes obvious once we remember that many of them were deeply involved with the threat of Gnosticism, and that Gnosticism was based almost entirely on the principle of divine revelation. What is a Gnostic? Someone who *knows*. And that knowledge has been revealed to them, and to them alone, in secret communications and esoteric instructions by a divine or semi-divine revealer. This, as we have seen, is something that the Apologists would not countenance for a moment. On the contrary, said they—especially Irenaeus and Clement of Alexandria—the true Gnostic is the Christian, the true Teacher is Christ, and the True Gnosticism is the Christian tradition. It is only to be expected, therefore, that Christ the Teacher, Christ the Revealer, Christ the Illuminator looms large in their writings.

Yet that is not all they have to say. Justin, the most influential of the group, anticipates all the other 'theories' or aspects which we noted above. He sees Christ as the Second Adam, restoring a creation which had been seriously damaged by the sins of the First Adam. This is the theory of recapitulation which we discussed in Chapter VIII (Irenaeus properly credits Justin with the idea) and it involves both Christ as Restorer and Christ as Victor. He recognizes that in his life and death Christ has overcome the Devil and his demons and has removed us all from their grasp, and he sees the cross as the chief symbol of his power. Nor is he in any doubt that he suffered for us, took our sins upon himself, and died that we might be forgiven: ideas which, as we shall see, involve both Christ as Victor and Christ as Victim. But in Justin, all these concepts are presented in their infancy. He does not develop them at length—we would hardly expect him to do so, given his time and his intentions (we talked about this in Chapter

III)—and their elaboration and refinement were to be the work of later generations of Christian theologians.

Christ as Restorer is a particularly Platonic idea. The principle is simple: when he became human, Christ took upon himself true and complete human nature; by taking this human nature upon himself he thereby transformed it and sanctified it; and by this transformation and sanctification, human nature, which had been rendered corruptible and mortal by the Fall, once again became capable of incorruption and immortality. Why is this idea particularly Platonic? Because Platonists prefer to think in terms of abstract universals rather than concrete particulars. We discussed this in Chapter II. They are happier dealing with 'Chairness' than with the particular chair on which you are sitting now; they would rather discuss 'The Cat' or 'Cats' than a particular feline called Rumbelow or Shinsilver; and they prefer to speak of 'Humanity' rather than David Bell or Jane Doe. For the Platonists, therefore, it was more natural to see the incarnation as the uniting of universal God with universal humanity, rather than the uniting of the universal God with the individual Jesus, the Galilean Son of Mary.

When we consider that the Platonic outlook was characteristic of a multitude of Greek fathers from Justin Martyr to Cyril of Alexandria (and, eventually, to Gregory Palamas and Nicholas Cabasilas in the fourteenth century), we will appreciate just how important and how widespread this principle was. But when we consider that in the west it was always less dominant, and eventually, in the later Middle Ages, was superseded by the views of Aristotle, who preferred particulars to universals, we will appreciate that the western emphasis was bound to be rather different.

The idea of the incarnational restoration of human nature lies at the root of two important theories of Christian progress: the theory of recapitulation and the theory of human deification or divinization. Of the former we need say little since it has already been considered in Chapter VIII, but the Platonic viewpoint is clear for all to see. With the disobedience, sinfulness, and so on, of the First Adam, 'Humanity' fell; with the obedience and sinlessness of the Second Adam, 'Humanity' was restored. The restoration was not restricted to Jesus of Nazareth, but was communicated to the whole race. In the incarnation, God became *human*, not just a particular man. He has therefore restored to all of us what we lost with Adam's Fall. What did we lose? For the easterners, the most important loss was the loss of our immortality and incorruption; for the westerners, and especially the westerners after Augustine, the most important loss was the loss of human innocence. But then the western view of human nature was always more pessimistic than that of the east.

The restoration of immortality and incorruption really lies at the heart of the doctrine of deification. 'God became human that in him we might become god': so said Athanasius (we quoted the saying earlier on page 81). But what does it mean 'to become god'? For the Christian church, it did not and could not mean that a human individual became identical with the Creator. This was never countenanced. Instead, if we may borrow the terminology of a much later medieval writer (William of Saint Thierry), it meant that one became, not God, but 'what God is.' That is to say, one was able to experience and share in the *attributes* or *qualities* of God, and the most important of these attributes were his blessedness, incorruption, and immortality.

In the beginning we were created in the image and likeness of God. What does this mean? It obviously does not apply to our physical forms, for despite the conventions of religious art, God does not have a long grey beard and a larger-than-usual human body. For us, here and now, the image is to be found in our rationality, our human capacity for abstract reasoning which distinguishes us from the animals (I do not myself believe this, by the way, but it is the standard Christian tradition), but in the case of

Adam, the situation was very different. Before the Fall he was immortal, as God is immortal, and incorrupt, as God is incorrupt. Something, therefore, has been lost, yet something has also been retained. It is true that we are now mortal, corruptible, and sinful, but we are still rational—the fathers expressed this by saying that the likeness has been lost while the image has remained—and by the use of this reason, in cooperation with grace, we may progress along the path which ultimately leads to salvation. Now, says Athanasius (and a host of others), with the incarnational transformation of human nature, the image has been restored: humankind can once again become immortal, incorruptible, sinless, and full of the knowledge of God—although, of course, the plenitude of this can only be experienced in the world to come. Redemption is therefore re-creation (you can see here how the old recapitulation theme has been raised to a new and better life), and by being 'deified' we are being re-formed to the stature of 'Humanity' (not just the man Adam) before the Fall.

This is certainly an impressive and optimistic doctrine, yet two important questions arise from it: firstly, is it an automatic and universal restoration—that is, does everyone benefit from it, whether pagan or Christian, saint or sinner, whether they want to or not—and secondly, if restoration was effected simply by the entry of Christ into the world, what need was there for his death and resurrection? The answer to the first question—and here we must speak generally, though not too inaccurately—is that the *possibility* of divinization is offered to all, but not all will take advantage of it. Who will take advantage? For western Augustinians, those who are predestined to do so; for easterners, non-Augustinians, and heretical Semi-Pelagians, those who, by their own free-will, in cooperation with grace, decide to do so. And since grace normally operates only within the church (we shall consider this fully in our next chapter), the effects of restoration and re-creation are, in practice, limited to Christians.

The answer to the second question becomes clear once we remember that not only are we subject to disease and corruption as a consequence of Adam/Humanity's sin, but are also doomed to die. 'Dust you are,' said God to Adam, 'and to dust you shall return' (Gen 3:19). Thus, because we all share in the sin of Adam and have ourselves sinned from Eden onwards, we are all under sentence of death. Humanity sinned; Humanity was condemned; Humanity must die. Humanity,therefore, *did* die; but it was not we who were executed, but the *Second Adam*. It was Christ, the *New* Humanity, who bore our sins, paid our debt, released us from God's condemnation, and thereby enabled us to benefit from the effects of his restoration. The Platonist viewpoint is here essential: Christ on the cross is not just Jesus, the son of Mary: he is Humanity itself. We-in-Christ achieve immortality as we-in-Adam were rendered mortal. Hence Athanasius: 'God became human that *in him* we might become god.' The death of Christ, therefore, enables us to benefit from Christ's transformation of humanity, and without it we would be like someone who decides to refurbish a house, put in new windows, buy new curtains and new carpets, purchase a new washer and dryer, and clean and paint everywhere in the full knowledge that the house has been expropriated by the local zoning board to make way for a new freeway and that the bulldozers will be moving in next week.

The crucifixion, then, was wholly necessary if we were to be released from sin and death—the fathers were agreed on that—but just how was the release accomplished? What precisely happened in those agonizing hours when the Second Adam died? Let us consider the answer of Gregory of Nyssa. According to Gregory, Adam sinned of his own free-will, and as a consequence it was by its own free-will that Humanity fell into the clutches of Satan. The Devil therefore has certain rights over us and, as we saw a moment ago, could justly demand our deaths. This, however, was not in accordance with God's plan, so he determined to deceive the Devil. In place of humankind he offered him instead his own Son incarnate, and when Satan saw Jesus in all his perfection and power and sinlessness he decided that the exchange would be much to his advantage, and he agreed. But unfortunately for Satan, he had not realized that concealed by the robe of flesh was the second person of the Trinity, true God, consubstantial with the Father, omnipotent, omniscient, eternal, unchangeable, immortal. Or, using Gregory's own somewhat unpleasing metaphor: the greedy fish (the Devil) gulped down the bait of the flesh and found himself caught on the hook of the Divinity.

When this happened, all hell broke loose (this is a nice opportunity to use the phrase literally). Christ the Victorious Victim conquered death, which, of course, had no hold over God. He descended into hell, where he preached to the 'spirits in prison' (1 Peter 3:19) and overthrew the power of the demons, binding the Devil hand and foot. An early apocryphal gospel even tells us what the demons said: 'Woe to us,' they cried, 'we have been defeated!' The ransom for Humanity was paid; death was overthrown; Satan was deceived, conquered, and bound; and from the depths of hell Christ arose triumphant.

This theory of the Devil's deception was not new with Gregory. Traces of it can be found far back in the second century and it is perfectly clear in the work of Origen (whom Gregory esteemed). Yet Gregory's imagery of bait and hook was not to everyone's taste (it is, on the whole, not much to ours either) and the whole theory of deceiving the Devil raised two important questions: firstly, whether the transaction was really ethical, and secondly, whether the Devil really had any rights at all.

Later fathers therefore amended the scheme slightly: they were in no doubt that the human race had sinned and that as a consequence it had put itself in Satan's power, but Satan, instead of just sitting back and counting souls, decided to help the matter along with some positive interference: he therefore seduced Judas and assailed Jesus. But since the latter was actually sinless, any assault upon him was contrary to divine law, and Satan had thereby over-reached himself. Because he had gone beyond his permitted bounds he was therefore just as guilty as humankind, and because he had abused his powers, whatever happened to him was just and right and proper. And as to whether he had rights, the fathers were, on the whole, agreed: he had rights only because God permitted him to have them.

However ethical or unethical was the theory of the Devil's deception, the later fathers never lost sight of the event which lay at the heart of the matter: the death of Christ. Christ was the ransom, the sacrifice, the substitute, and according to Gregory of Nazianzus (and others), when he was crucified, our sins were crucified with him. This was not just a formal acknowledgement of the fact. For the later fathers the death of Christ was an event of real and momentous significance, and when Basil the Great says that the price for all mankind was paid in 'the holy and most precious blood of our Lord Jesus Christ,' he really means what he says. Despite their concern with restoration and deification, the later eastern fathers never lost sight of this crucial event, and despite a tendency to conceal the cross with a wealth of elaborate symbolism, they never denied the necessity of the bloody sacrifice which took place upon it.

The importance of the crucifixion, however,—of Christ as Victim—was even more marked in the west. We have already seen that Tertullian regarded it as the central event of Christianity and that in his view it contained within itself the whole essence of the tradition. It was he, too, who introduced the term 'satisfaction'—*satisfactio* in Latin—and although he himself did not use it with reference to the work of Christ (Cyprian may have been the first to do so, and his approach is tentative and cautious), later Latin writers welcomed it as the best expression for the payment

of the penalty due to God because of human sin. This is not
to deny that the other aspects we have considered also
played a role in western theology: Christ as Teacher was of
great importance for Clement of Rome as well as for Tertullian (Tertullian was also well acquainted with recapitulation theory); Christ as Restorer and 'Deifier' was not
neglected, although this aspect of his work is elaborated
more by those who, like Hilary, the bilingual bishop of
Poitiers (the 'Athanasius of the West' whom we mentioned
earlier in Chapter VII), were more deeply influenced by the
world of Alexandria and Constantinople; the theory of the
Devil's deception was widely accepted; but it was above all
on Christ as Victim that western theology concentrated.

> 'He died that we might be forgiven,
> He died to make us good,
> That we might go at last to heaven,
> Saved by his precious blood.'

This famous Victorian hymn is the authentic voice of the
Latin west, and the western answer to the question 'Why
did God become human?' could well be 'Because he had to
die.' To some extent this is a simplification of the more
metaphysical theories of the Greek east. It is an easy doctrine to understand: we are guilty; we are condemned to
death; someone else pays the price ('It is a far, far better
thing that I do . . .'); it is accepted; we are released. This, as
we know, is the thought of Tertullian, and it also reflects
the thought of a long line of formulators of western doctrine who were more often hard-headed administrators
rather than speculative theologians. On the other hand, as
the genius of Augustine makes clear, this is not all that the
west had to say. He, as usual, was able to perceive and
draw together all the threads we have so far considered
and weave them into a comprehensive and coherent doctrine.

Augustine never forgets Christ as Teacher, but he is a teacher who teaches more by his example than by his words. As the living embodiment of love, he shows us how to love; and as the most astonishing example of humility (this is *God*, after all, who has emptied himself and become human), he teaches us how to be humble. According to Augustine, there are three steps on the path which leads to redemption: the first step is humility; the second step is humility; and the third step is humility.

Nor does he forget Christ as Restorer, but his approach to this aspect is more typically western than eastern. He does indeed say that God became human to make humans gods, but that is not where his real interest lies. His Restorer is the Mediator, the one true Mediator, who, because he is truly God and truly human, brings God down to us and raises us up to God. In his own person he bridges the gap which Adam opened and restores God and humanity to its right relationship. This is the atonement in the literal sense: the restored 'at-one-ment' of the Creator and his creation.

We also see in his work copious examples of Christ as Victor over the Devil and his demons. But Augustine is well aware of the problems raised by Gregory of Nyssa and other similar thinkers, and although he sometimes uses imagery similar to that of Gregory's fish (Satan, he says, was caught by the lure of Christ's body like a mouse 'taking the bait in a mousetrap'), his own view of the matter is subtly different. When humanity sinned, it certainly passed into the power of the Devil; but this does not mean that the Devil had any absolute rights. He was *permitted* by God to take us into his power. But because he had no rights in the matter, neither could he demand any ransom; and what this means, in turn, is that the death of Christ was not, in itself, any payment made to the Devil. With his death, the Second Adam restored the creation which had been deformed by the First Adam, and once again united Creator and creation. In this the Devil had no say. He may not have liked it, but there was nothing he could have done about it. The crucifixion would then have released the souls he had in his care whether he liked it or not, and for all his anger and fury, he could not have prevented them from walking out of his domain through the door which Christ had opened. But God is a just God, and to give the Devil no choice in the matter seemed not consonant with divine justice. So God delivered up his Son to death, and the Devil, in his greed and malice, could not resist reaching out and taking him. And then, because he had taken a sinless victim, the Devil himself was caught. He had over-stepped his appointed bounds and was therefore as guilty as the human souls he had in his care. 'Right,' said God, 'in payment for *your* sin, I require the return of humanity,' and Satan then had no choice but to deliver it up.

In other words, it was the crucifixion itself, not any ransom paid to the Devil, which brought about our release, remission, and redemption, and the 'deception' of the Devil only resulted in his being required by law to do something which he would have had to do anyway. It is the crucifixion itself which is central for the western Augustine: 'By his death, the one most true sacrifice offered for us, he purged, abolished, extinguished whatever guilt there was by which the principalities and powers (i.e., the demons) were justly holding us fast to pay its penalty.'[1] Nor is this an isolated passage, and with the ideas and authority of Tertullian and Augustine at its source and as its foundation it is hardly surprising that Christ as the Victorious Victim came to represent the dominant strain of western thinking on the redemption.

It is clear, however, that neither in east nor west do we have four separate theories as to how salvation works. There are not four separate answers to the question '*Cur Deus Homo*?' Christ as Teacher, Restorer, Victor, and Victim is one and the same Christ, and although the emphases

---

[1] Augustine of Hippo, *De Trinitate* 4.13.17.

change, all four factors interact and concur. East and west, naturally, stress different aspects. Why should they not? They represent, after all, different peoples with different cultures, different languages, and different outlooks. But neither denied or wished to deny that the whole of Christ's life was necessary and that his birth, teaching, example, death, resurrection, and ascension were all alike essential for the fulfilment of the divine plan. By his incarnation as a whole—not just by one single part of it—we are redeemed, and by God's grace we are able to enjoy all the benefits of this redemption. We must now turn, therefore, to a discussion of just how these benefits might be obtained and where they are most effectively to be found. In other words, we turn from the incarnate body of Christ to the mystical body of Christ: to the doctrine of the Christian church.

OLD SAINT PETER'S CHURCH, ROME. Adapted from a
sixteenth-century painting in the Vatican.

CHAPTER XIV

ONE AND HOLY: THE MYSTICAL BODY OF CHRIST

T HE CHURCH WAS ALWAYS CONVINCED that it was the receptacle of grace, and without wishing to limit the almighty powers of God, it was equally convinced that under normal circumstances, salvation was not to be found outside it. Cyprian, the third-century bishop of Carthage, put the matter in a nutshell: 'Someone who does not have the Church as mother cannot have God as father.'[1] Augustine, likewise, was in no doubt. He knew that exceptions did occur—there was the obvious case of the centurion Cornelius in Acts 10—but such exceptions were rare. If the normal, visible means of grace were available, the believer was expected to use it: the church was not just a convenient, but a *necessary* part of the process of salvation. It was not just a social group, a society of believers, but the mystical body of Christ. This was a concept of first importance for all the fathers, both eastern and western, for as

---

[1]Cyprian, *De unitate ecclesiae* 6.

Christ united himself with our humanity in the incarnation, so we are united with him as members of his mystical body. As members of the church we are incorporated—the word means literally 'put into the body'—in Christ, and as Christ himself is eternal and indestructible, so, too, is his mystical body. As Christ fulfilled the promises of the Old Testament, so also is his mystical body the fulfillment of those promises: it is the true Israel, the eschatological society, and, as we are told in the 'Constantinopolitan' Creed, it is one, holy, universal, and apostolic.

What do these terms mean, and how can they be defended as descriptions of a church which was continually racked by heresy and schism, which was often led by men of manifestly mixed motives and devious designs, and which, on many occasions, did not appear to be particularly holy?

Let us begin by considering the church in its oneness, for this will lead us in turn to a discussion of the other three concepts. At the most obvious level, since Christ has only one body, so there can be only one church, and all other ideas are, in essence, derived from this. There is one baptism into the one body, one faith in the one Lord, one belief in the one God, and as Christ united himself with us because of his love for us, so it is love which unites us with him and ourselves with each other: 'We love, because he first loved us' (1 John 4:19). The church is one in mutual love, said Augustine: love is its life-blood; but he was not the first to say this, and the idea has a history going right back to the New Testament.

What, then, are we to say of the heretics and schismatics? By separating themselves from the church (the schismatics) or by denying its doctrines (the heretics), they have imperilled both its unity and its universality and have turned their backs on the vessel of grace. But are we to regard them in exactly the same light as pagans, Jews, Zoroastrians, Gnostics, and other perverted unfortunates? Putting it another way, is there any difference between a person who has never known, liked, or been associated with Christianity, and someone who was born into a Christian family, was baptized, attended church regularly, but then, because (let us say) they found Pelagianism more attractive than orthodoxy, found themselves outside the Christian fold in an attempt to live a Christian life?

Let us consider the case of Novatian. Born about 200, Novatian was an intelligent and acute theologian, the author of an excellent, orthodox, and neglected treatise on the Trinity, and the chief presbyter of the Roman church. In the year 250, he and all other Christians found themselves subjected to a vicious and systematic persecution instigated by the emperor Decius, and during the eighteen months of terror (the persecution ended in June 251 with Decius' death) a considerable number of Christians had apostatized—i.e., had denied Christianity and saved their lives by making the requisite offerings to the pagan gods— and many others, by simple bribery, had been able to obtain from the civil authorities official documents which stated that they had sacrificed, when, in fact, they had not. What was to be done with these people once the persecution was over, when many of them wished to return to the church, and many others—those who had simply bought the necessary documents—could say, with some justification, that they had never really left it?

Novatian was at first fairly lenient and farsighted with regard to these individuals, but then, partly because of his own austere theology, but mainly because of his determined opposition to and dislike of Pope Cornelius I (who was also lenient, but who had been elected to the position Novatian himself had coveted), he joined the more rigorous party who maintained that once you were out of the church you were out forever, and that there was no possible way back in. Novatian then had himself consecrated as an anti-pope to Cornelius, and the Novatianist sect spread rapidly and achieved considerable importance. Its organization was precisely the same as that of the orthodox church, and with one exception its doctrinal teachings were identical: the only difference was that the Novatians did not think that there was any forgiveness for major sins committed after baptism. For this belief they were excommunicated.

What we have here, then, are schismatics who are orthodox Christians in all matters but one. Are we really to consider them as no better than pagans? According to Cyprian of Carthage, Novatian's contemporary, the answer to that question is Yes. So far as he was concerned, all those outside the church were to be considered in precisely the same light, and there was no essential difference between a Novatian schismatic and the emperor Decius himself. Furthermore, if any of the Novatians had received baptism from Novatian clergy, that baptism was invalid, and if any of these people eventually saw the light and expressed a desire to join the official, true, orthodox, universal church—Cyprian's church—then they would have to be rebaptized.

This point of view was thought by many to be far too harsh, and one of those who thought it too harsh was Pope Stephen I, who had ascended the papal throne in May 254. It was the Roman practice to readmit those who had apostatized simply by giving them an appropriate penance (though we should note that at this time in the church's history, such penance could be very long and extremely arduous), and to receive those who had been baptized by the Novatians—or any other schismatic Christians—simply by giving them absolution by the laying on of hands. The great metropolitan see of Alexandria and most of the Palestinian churches agreed with Rome in this matter, but North Africa (Cyprian's homeland), Syria, and most of Asia Minor did not. Cyprian certainly did not. Like his predecessor Tertullian (whom he esteemed), he considered heretical baptism to be totally invalid and was quite prepared to oppose the pope in saying so. As a consequence, the church was faced with the threat of a major division, with the Romans and their allies on one side and the North Africans and their friends on the other. That this split did not occur was the consequence not of diplomacy but of death: Stephen died in August of 257 and Cyprian in September of 258, and with the departure from the scene of the two principal protagonists in the controversy, the situation gradually stabilized. But the dispute brings to light two very important questions: (1) what is the relationship of the church of Rome to the other churches, and (2) what makes a sacrament valid?

The church had always believed that it was 'apostolic.' That is to say, it was sure that it was built on the foundation of the prophets and the apostles, and that the chief cornerstone was Christ himself (Eph 2:20). This was stressed particularly by the second-century writers in their struggle with Gnosticism—we discussed the case of Irenaeus of Lyons in Chapter III—who insisted that the true tradition of the church was not to be found in secret gospels and esoteric teachings, but in the visible and public tradition handed down from the apostles to their successors. Hence Tertullian could say that although there were many great churches, they were all really the first church, that which was founded by the apostles and from which all of them derived. 'In this way all are primitive and apostolic.'[2] Who, then, were the successors of the apostles? In the earliest writings we find no clear distinction between the presbyteral and episcopal offices, but it was not long before the bishops, and the bishops alone, were seen as the inheritors of the apostolic powers and responsibilities. It was for them (if we may use the terminology of a later age) to preach the gospel, govern the church, and administer the sacraments. We see the beginnings of this idea in the writings of Ignatius of Antioch (whom we metin Chapter III), who saw in the bishop the symbol of the

---

[2]Tertullian, *De praescriptione haereticorum* 20.

church's unity, and we see it infinitely more clearly in the letters and treatises of Cyprian of Carthage.

Cyprian has no doubt that each individual bishop is master in his own diocese and that each individual bishop is answerable to God alone. Secondly, he takes the ideas of Ignatius much further and is prepared to state categorically that since the bishop is in the church and the church in the bishop, then if you are not with the bishop, you are not with the church. Thirdly, the bishops together form a college, and each member of this college enjoys the powers of the whole college, so that when any one speaks, he speaks with the authority of the whole apostolic church behind him. What, then, of Rome? The bishop of Rome, says Cyprian, like every other bishop, may speak with this authority, but—and it is a very important 'but'—no one is entitled to set himself up as a 'bishop of bishops' and force his colleagues to compulsory obedience. In other words, Cyprian is perfectly willing to ascribe to Rome a primacy of *honour*, but not a primacy of *jurisdiction*. If the bishops were to meet in synod, Rome might naturally take the chair, but when it came to the vote, the Roman vote would count no more and no less than any other vote, and if Rome were outvoted, that was that.

The view of Rome itself was rather different. From an early period its bishops had assumed that they had a greater authority than that of any other bishop, even though the other bishops had not been prepared to accept it. We saw in Chapter III how Clement, at the very end of the first century, was quite prepared to remonstrate with the church at Corinth, and late in the second century, Pope Victor I (the first Latin pope, by the way) had tried to impose his will on the churches of Asia Minor who celebrated Easter on the precise day of the Jewish Passover and not (as was the Roman practice) on the Sunday following. He did not succeed, that is true, but his attempt shows clearly that in his view, Rome had a perfect right to intervene in the affairs of another diocese. Pope Stephen, Cyprian's adversary, agreed totally with this, and based his claim on the famous Petrine text in Matthew 16:18: 'You are Peter, and on this rock I will build my church'—he was the first pope we know of who did so. And despite the fact that Cyprian and others like him disagreed radically with this conception, it gradually gained wider and wider acceptance in the west—especially through the efforts of popes like Damasus I and Innocent I—until, in the second half of the fifth century, Leo the Great took all the ideas which had developed thus far, melded them together, added further material to them, and produced a cohesive doctrine of the Roman primacy which was to become the accepted viewpoint of the western church until the Second Vatican Council. According to Leo, supreme authority was given to Peter by Christ, and Peter was the first bishop of Rome. This supreme authority is therefore transmitted only to those who follow him as bishops of Rome, and the authority of other bishops is transmitted to them from Christ *through Peter*, and not from Christ directly. Hence, whereas the authority of other bishops is limited to their own dioceses, the supreme authority of the bishop of Rome— 'Peter Revivified'—extends over the whole church, and the bishop of Rome is the ultimate source of authority and doctrine. In this way, too, the universality of the church could easily be discerned, for what could be a more obvious manifestation of this universality than the acknowledgement by all the churches of a single source of authority, and the universal acceptance of the Roman standard?

These ideas, though eventually accepted by the western churches, were never accepted by those in the east. Their view was essentially the same as that of Cyprian: one man, one vote; and although there was never any doubt that Rome was the first and most honourable see of Christendom, and that the bishop of Rome was *primus inter pares*, 'first among equals,' the eastern churches never ascribe— and never have ascribed—to him any more than a primacy of honour. It was inevitable, therefore, that sometime in the future east and west would clash on this point, and clash they did; but the story of that collision, and how it came to play a major role in the Great Schism of 1054, is a matter outside the scope of our present investigation.

Let us now turn to the second problem which arose from the dispute of Stephen and Cyprian: the question of the validity of the sacraments. To understand this—and its ultimate resolution —we must investigate yet another controversy: that of the Donatists. This began in 311 with the consecration of a new bishop of Carthage. Yet it was not the new bishop who caused the problems; it was the bishop who consecrated him. The latter had been caught up in the persecution of the emperor Diocletian and, to save his skin, had surrendered copies of the scriptures to the pagan authorities. According to his opponents, by so doing he had apostatized, and because he had apostatized, he was outside the church and his episcopal rank was forfeited; and because these opponents were of the same opinion as Cyprian—i.e., they believed that only sacraments celebrated within the church are valid—they denied that the new bishop had been validly consecrated, and they refused to recognize him. Instead they consecrated one of their own party as bishop, and he was very soon succeeded by Donatus, from whom the heresy is named.

The Donatists were rigorists: in many ways they were similar to the austere Novatians, and their hero was Cyprian. But not only did they deny that sacraments celebrated by unworthy ministers were invalid, they also maintained that the church, the body of Christ and the bride of Christ (Christian theology can produce some very curious sexual relationships), should be preserved spotless and immaculate, and that its holiness was to be found in the holiness of its individual members. On this score the Donatists were the Puritans of the early church, demanding perfection of all the faithful, and asserting, in consequence, that sinners were not part of the church. Their views were condemned by their orthodox Roman rivals, but the schismatics persisted and grew in strength, partly because they claimed Cyprian as their main authority (and Cyprian was highly regarded in North Africa) and partly because they fed on anti-Roman North African nationalism which, at the time, could arouse very violent emotions.

Opposition to Donatism came first from Optatus, a North African bishop of whose life we know nothing whatsoever, and then, more importantly, from Augustine, who developed the ideas of Optatus and established a number of extremely important principles. First of all, asked Augustine (and Optatus), who effects a sacrament? It is certainly not the officiating presbyter. Baptism, for example, is carried out in the name of the Father, Son, and Holy Spirit, not in the name of John Smith or Bishop Donatus. It is *God* who effects the sacraments, who makes them work, and the officiating minister is no more than a channel for this divine grace. For someone dying of thirst it matters little whether the person who carries them water is clean or dirty: the essential thing is not the bearer, but the water. Similarly, since the author of any sacrament is the omnipotent God, then if the sacrament is celebrated in accordance with the tradition of the church, the worthiness or unworthiness of the minister is wholly irrelevant. Indeed, if this were not the case, we could be in deep trouble. How do you know whether or not a priest is in a state of sin? And if you cannot be sure of this (and the priest is hardly going to tell you), then you cannot ever be sure of whether the sacrament is valid or whether it is not. And to have the validity of any sacrament dependent on a totally unknown quantity is a ridiculous and intolerable situation.

So is there any difference at all between baptism performed by, say, a Novatian or Donatist and baptism performed by the pope? Yes and no, says Augustine, for we need to distinguish a sacrament asleep from a sacrament awake. Or, in more theological terms, we need to distinguish the validity of a sacrament from its efficacy. A baptized Donatist has truly been baptized, but the gift of baptism is dormant or sleeping; for it to awake and bring about all the effects which baptism does bring about (rebirth into the true body of Christ, washing off of past sins, communication of grace—matters we shall consider in our final chapter), the Donatist must leave Donatism and seek entry into the orthodox church. Once there, the sacrament 'works' or wakes up or becomes effective, for only in the one true church, the one body of Christ, is salvation to be found. With this theory Augustine produced a neat compromise between the Roman and North African positions: schismatic sacraments are valid, but not efficacious; because they are valid, they do not need to be repeated (which agrees with Pope Stephen), but because they are not efficacious, their recipient, if he or she remains outside the church, is still doomed (which agrees with Cyprian).

For those who join the universal church, and for those already in it, salvation is offered freely. But to whom is it offered? Listen to St Paul: 'Christ Jesus came into the world to save sinners' (1 Tim. 1:15); he did not come to save the perfect. The Donatists' view of the holiness of the church is therefore utterly wrong. The church is not a society of saints, but a Noah's ark (the analogy is an old one) in which are to be found all manner of beasts, both, clean and unclean. The holiness of the church, said Augustine, was not to be found in the holiness of its individual members, but in the holiness of the holy grace which was mediated through its sacraments. Its holiness, therefore, was not something created by its human members, but something bestowed upon it by its divine Lord. It was an objective, not a subjective holiness.

On the other hand, Augustine could not deny that there was some truth in the Donatist claim that the Body and Bride of Christ should be as pure as possible, and as a consequence of his intimate familiarity with Later Platonic thought and its clear-cut distinction of the ideal from the actual, he was able to accommodate this idea within his own doctrine. He therefore distinguished the essential, inner church from the outward and visible church. The former is composed of those individuals who are truly aflame with the fire of charity, who are filled with the Spirit of love (which is the Holy Spirit, the mutual love of Father and Son, as we saw in Chapter VII), and who are utterly devoted to their Lord, in body, soul, and spirit. It is these who are the Body of Christ in the proper sense, and it is these who constitute the society of the saints. The others make up the visible church—your average Christians, in other words—and although they are truly its members and although the sacraments are efficacious for them, they are, in a sense *in* the church, but not *of* it. They are not the spiritual élite.

A little later, when Augustine had become so deeply involved in the Pelagian controversy, he was able to add a refinement to this concept: the true, essential church now becomes the company of the predestined, the society of the elect, and its numbers accordingly correspond to the numbers of the angels who fell with Satan. This, of course, reintroduces all the problems of predestinationism which we discussed briefly in Chapter XII, and if we take the idea to its logical conclusion it raises the very nasty question of whether there is any point at all in the visible and imperfect church in which so many Christians take such an interest. Augustine, perhaps wisely, never pursues the theme, and the essential point of his argument is not the *identity* of the righteous saints, but the fact that they will not be known until the Last Judgment at the end of the world. Only then will the sheep be separated from the goats, and only God knows which is which. The Donatists, in trying to establish a sheep-only church in this present time, are anticipating the Last Judgment and claiming for themselves the sort of discrimination which belongs only to the Creator.

The essence of the church, says Augustine, is not the outward holiness of its members, but the love they have for one another. Love, the Holy Spirit, is the life-blood of the church —we said so at the beginning of this chapter—and you cannot be a member of the church (and you cannot therefore be a true Christian) without truly loving God and your fellow Christians. This love is something manifestly lacking among the Donatists, and for Augustine, the reason they are outside the church is not their doctrinal inaccuracies or theological disagreements, but their lack of charity. We might observe, of course, that there was also a conspicuous lack of charity on the part of the anti-Donatist party, particularly after Augustine came to accept as valid the idea of coercion (the principle, based on Luke 14:23, that if the schismatics will not return to the one, true church of their own free will, they may be forced to return, whether they want to or not), but given the nature of fallen humanity this is not too surprising. It has always been a truism—at least until the Viet-Nam War—that only the enemy ever commits war crimes.

Western theology after Augustine had little to add to his doctrine of the church. There was certainly a development in the idea of the Roman primacy (we traced it above from Clement I to Leo I), but in its essentials, Augustine's doctrine became the officially accepted teaching of the orthodox west. The church was one in the love of God and one's neighbour; it was holy in the holy grace of the Holy Spirit; it dispensed valid sacraments regardless of the worthiness or unworthiness of the minister; it was the outward and visible form—the institutional form—of an essential inner church; it included both sinners and righteous, who would be separated only at the Last Judgment; it was a church whose teachings and traditions began with Christ and his apostles and were then transmitted from generation to generation by its bishops, the successors of the apostles; and outside of this church there was no salvation. To this must be added the Leonine contribution—accepted only in the west—that the universality of the church could be seen in the universal acknowledgement of Rome and its bishop as the seat and source of supreme authority.

In the orthodox east, the situation, as we might expect, was rather different. The controversies we have examined (Novatianism and Donatism) and nearly all the protagonists (Cyprian, Novatian, Donatus, Optatus, Tertullian, Stephen, Victor, Cornelius, Damasus, Innocent, Leo, Augustine) were western, and it is controversy which gives rise to doctrine. The easterners, therefore, tended to repeat old and well-established ideas—the church as the True Israel, as the Bride of Christ, as the vessel of the Holy Spirit, and so on—and although it is possible to find all of Augustine's ideas (but not Rome's claim to primacy of jurisdiction) echoed by Greek writers, the eastern church (or, more precisely, the eastern church before the Great Schism of 1054) never produced—never needed to produce—a consistent and comprehensive ecclesiology. Its main focus of interest lay with the church as the Body of Christ, the incorporation of the faithful into this body, and, as a consequence, their 'deification' or 'divinization.' How was this 'incorporation' achieved? Most especially through participation in the eucharist, the most dramatic of the sacraments, and it is to this drama and its significance that we must now turn.

BAPTISM by immersion. Adapted from a ninth-century manuscript.

EUCHARIST. Adapted from a third-century fresco in Rome.

CHAPTER XV

THE COMMUNICATION OF GRACE

THE FATHERS OF THE CHURCH were universally convinced that in a sacrament or mystery (the former term is Latin; the latter, Greek) we have the outward and visible sign of an inward and spiritual grace. They might not have expressed the idea in these words, nor have been quite sure as to how the two realities were connected, but the principle was accepted by all parties. It is, however, a fairly broad principle, and could obviously be applied to a large number of visible signs. Repetition of the creed, for example, could be the audible sign of an inner faith, and this inner faith itself was a consequence of sanctifying grace. The creed, therefore, could be called a sacrament, and is so called by Augustine. Not until the twelfth century do we find the standard and formal list of seven sacraments—Baptism, Confirmation, Eucharist, Penance, Unction, Ordination, Matrimony—which was to become the traditional teaching of the Roman church, and, by being borrowed from it at a still later date, of the eastern churches as well.

Yet despite the broad significance of the term and the possibility of several dozen sacraments, four came to be generally considered outstanding in their importance: the inseparable combination of baptism and confirmation, penance (particularly in the west), and, of course, the eucharist.

In baptism one died to one's old life, one was buried with Christ, and one rose again from the tomb of the waters to a new life in and with one's Saviour. Just as the whole body is buried, so the whole body is immersed, and it was not until the early Middle Ages that the western church began to adopt its present practice of affusion or infusion, in which the water is poured only over the head of a child. The earlier church insisted—and the eastern churches still insist—that without total immersion (so far as is practicable) the symbolism—the 'sign'—is incomplete. As a consequence of this baptismal rebirth, four things were thought to occur: Christ was accepted as Saviour; one entered the ark of salvation, the universal church; one's previous sins were washed away; and one received the grace of the Holy Spirit. These last two factors were naturally of first importance, but whereas the remission of sins applied equally to all (the fathers stressed this remission as a total remission for everybody: there were no little bits of sin left over), grace was received in proportion to one's own faith: the greater that faith, the greater the grace received.

Just when this grace was communicated, however, was not entirely clear to the fathers. Jerome had no doubt that it came with the baptismal immersion itself, and there were many who thought like him; but over the course of time it came to be generally accepted that whereas the baptism proper washed away sin, the communication of grace was effected after the candidate had climbed out of the font, had been anointed with holy oil, and had received the laying on of hands. Since the Greek word for this oil is 'chrism' (it was basically olive oil, to which a number of perfumes and spices could be added), the Greek churches refer to this rite as chrismation. The west, as we shall see in a moment, prefers the term confirmation. But although the eastern and western churches differed in the emphasis they placed on the two parts of the rite (the east stressed the anointing; the west, the laying on of hands), both were quite sure that it was essential and both insisted that it should follow immediately after immersion, just as the dove of the Holy Spirit descended on Christ immediately after he had arisen from the waters of the Jordan.

For some three centuries, the church restricted the administration of regular baptism to Easter or Pentecost, but recognized that in an emergency, it could be performed at any time. But with the rapid increase in the number of Christians in the wake of imperial approval in the course of the fourth century, epiphany also came to be considered an appropriate season, and then, from the fifth century onwards, against some formidable opposition (by Leo the Great, for example), Christmas and other major feasts were also thought suitable. But the increasing numbers of candidates affected not only the times of baptism, but the actual way in which the rite was conducted: in the earliest church, the bishop alone took responsibility for both baptism and chrismation, but with more and more candidates appearing and more and more churches to deal with, it gradually became logistically impossible for him to continue this one-man practice. What, then, was to be done? East and west (as usual) adopted somewhat different solutions. In the east, both baptism and chrismation passed into the hands of the local priest, and the bishop's role was restricted to the rite of consecrating the chrism before it was sent out to the local clergy (in modern Orthodoxy this consecration is further restricted to bishops who are the heads of autocephalous churches). In the west, only the rite of baptism passed to the local priest, and the laying on of hands remained an episcopal function; and since the bishop obviously could not be present at the baptism of every child, the laying on of hands tended to be delayed until there were sufficient candidates to warrant an episcopal visitation, or until the bishop had time to attend to the matter. In either case, this resulted in a delay between baptism and what came to be called confirmation, and this, in turn, demanded some investigation of precisely what happened on these two distinct occasions. If we maintain that baptism only removes sin and that grace is not communicated until the laying on of hands, then what happens to a child in the days, months, or years between the two ceremonies? In the east, of course, this was hardly a problem, for chrismation followed directly on baptism (it still does), and when the various effects occurred never became a question of major importance. Whatever was due to happen had certainly happened by the end of the single ceremony. But in the west this was not the case. Was the child left entirely graceless between the two rites? Or was it that grace was indeed communicated in the actual immersion (as Jerome said it was), but that the laying on of hands somehow aroused it further or strengthened it or *confirmed* it? It was, of course, this latter solution which the west was to adopt.

The idea of 'confirming' or strengthening, however, was not a western invention. It can be traced back to Greek writers of the late second century, and in the third and fourth centuries it received a gradually increasing emphasis. The actual Latin term —*confirmatio*—first appears in a western document from the middle of the fifth century, and the theory of what happens is clearly expressed in a Latin sermon which circulated very widely in the west and which was almost certainly written by a fifth-century cleric called Faustus, who was bishop of Riez (a diocese in the very south of France). According to Faustus, the grace of the Holy Spirit is indeed communicated during baptism, and if one were to die straightaway, that grace would be more than sufficient to ensure one's entry into the kingdom of heaven. But if one survives baptism and then goes on to live for many more years, additional help is necessary to fight the temptations and perils of life in this world. This is where confirmation comes in: it is the blessing of the Holy Spirit in which one is provided with the necessary spiritual weapons and the strength to use them; or, if we may use a more modern analogy, it is the booster shot which strengthens and renders fully effective a prior vaccination.

Let us turn now to the question of the age at which baptism should be administered. It is well known that the major churches of the west and all the churches of the east baptize in infancy, and in so doing they follow a tradition which may possibly—though not certainly—be traced right back to the New Testament. Be that as it may, there is no doubt that by the end of the second century infant baptism was not uncommon, and it spread fairly widely during the course of the third century. There was always considerable opposition to the practice, primarily from those who, like Tertullian in the west or Cyril of Jerusalem in the east, considered that conversion to Christianity was an undertaking of the utmost seriousness and that no one should be expected to shoulder its burdens (and receive its benefits) unless they were fully cognizant of what they were doing. On the other hand, there were also those—and they proved to be in the majority—who emphasized the great desirability of having a child a full and dedicated member of the church from as early a date as possible. Surely, if God's grace is indeed offered freely to us, we should make sure our children receive it at the earliest opportunity?

With the increasing numbers of infants born to Christian parents and with the development of the doctrine of penance, which could deal with post-baptismal sin (we shall speak of this in a moment), baptism of infants gradually became the norm, and the authority of Augustine in the west simply confirmed what, by his time, was effectively the standard practice. For Augustine, as we know, infants come into this world not just stained, but utterly corrupted by Adam's sin, and if they die uncleansed and unbaptized, they must therefore bear the consequences of this sin and go to hell. Augustine says so. Their punishment may be the lightest possible punishment, that is true, but they are still condemned to eternal torment (this obnoxious doctrine was qualified and mitigated in the Middle Ages, but that story lies outside the scope of our investigation). It was therefore essential, absolutely essential, for an infant to be baptized, and consequently cleansed of original sin, as soon as possible, and with the triumph of Augustinianism in the west, this became standard western doctrine. But since the east had never accepted the principle of total human depravity, the defenders of infant baptism there laid greater stress on the more positive aspects of the rite (incorporation into the body of Christ and the reception of sanctifying grace) rather than on those which were negative (the removal of original sin and the avoidance of hell).

On the other hand, no one denied that baptism did wash away sins, and once it had become established practice to baptize children, Christians could not avoid the problem of what to do about sins committed after baptism. In the late fourth century there appeared a small and heretical body within the church who thought that baptism not only cleansed one from sins past, but also prevented one from sinning in the future (if you read 1 Jn 3:9, you will see why), but the overwhelming orthodox opinion held that this was absolute rubbish, and that anyone who maintained it knew neither the scriptures nor humankind. One solution, of course, was to defer baptism to as late a date as possible (Constantine, for instance, who had sinned more spectacularly than most men, wisely delayed his baptism until he was almost dead), but this had to be balanced against the danger of sure damnation if one failed to get to the font on time.

To deal with the problem the church developed the doctrine of penance, and there is a wealth of material on the subject in texts from the later fourth century onwards. The Cappadocian Fathers, for example, provide copious information on the length and severity of penance, and they, with many others, sought to distinguish major sins (which certainly included apostasy, murder, and adultery) from those of lesser consequence. The schism of the Novatians, who refused to accept that there was any forgiveness at all for major sins committed after baptism, also forced the orthodox to look very seriously at the matter and not only to state, but also to defend, the contrary view. Penance came to be regarded as—and also termed—a 'second baptism,' and like the first baptism, it cleansed one from all the dross and filth and sin which one had accumulated up to the time it was undertaken. But like the first baptism, penance could only be performed once, and again like the first baptism, it was a public act. Sinners had to ask for penance from the bishop, and if this were granted, they were immediately excluded from the eucharist and had to undergo an extremely severe course of prayer and fasting for as long as the bishop thought necessary. For serious sins, such as incest or murder, it could last for years. Only after this gruelling period had been completed was the cleansed sinner restored to the congregation and to communion, and even then was doomed to life-long continence. It will not come as a surprise, therefore, to learn, firstly, that this 'second baptism' was normally deferred until one's deathbed and, secondly, that it was just too severe to last. In the late sixth century it began to collapse, and over the ensuing decades penances gradually became much more lenient and much more a formality; but that, again, is a matter outside the scope of our present study.

Baptism, chrismation, and penance were undoubtedly sacraments of the first importance, yet they were still very much 'signs' of a sacred reality. The water in the font remained water; the oil remained oil. No change occurred in their substantial nature. But in the eucharist, this was clearly not the case. In one sense the bread and wine were simply 'signs' or symbols of invisible grace, but in another they were true flesh and blood, and were therefore the

realities themselves. We may say at the outset that this was
something never denied by the fathers of the church and
never the subject of controversy. Disputes over the real
presence and transubstantiation and so on do not occur
until the ninth century, and Christian writers from Ignatius
of Antioch to Augustine had no difficulty in believing that
when Christ said 'This is my body,' that was precisely
what he meant. Neither did these writers see the slightest
incompatibility between viewing the bread and wine sometimes symbolically and sometimes realistically—the two
viewpoints were never seen as being in any way mutually
exclusive—and although we do find differences of emphasis (the early Alexandrians, as we might expect, were
the symbolists *par excellence*; the Antiochenes emphasized
that there was bread and flesh, flesh and bread, two distinct realities), everyone was agreed that in the eucharistic
rite a definite and undoubted change did occur. The first to
state this clearly may have been Justin, but he only echoes a
common idea, and although the early fathers had no standard terminology for the eucharistic miracle (for some it
'changed'; for others it 'was converted'; some saw it as
'refashioned'; others as 'transmuted'; and so on), nor any
precise theory as to how the change took place, they had
not the slightest difficulty in accepting it as an undeniable
and undisputed fact.

Justin also provides us with a fascinating—though incomplete—description of just what happened at a second-
century eucharist, and much of what he says would be
familiar material to practising Christians. But Justin's description also makes it quite clear that by his time, the
eucharist was intended to be not a full-scale but a token
meal, and that the convivial atmosphere of a dinner party
had given way to the more sombre and ritualistic aspect of
the church. The very earliest Christians seem not to have
made this distinction, and their *agapē* or 'love-feast' was a
reenactment of the real and substantial meal taken by
Christ with his disciples before his execution. You ate and

drank to fill yourself at these occasions; you rejoiced and gave thanks ('thanksgiving' is what 'eucharist' means); and as is clear from the problems Paul had to face in Corinth (see 1 Cor 7–8 and 11:20–34), the rejoicing could sometimes get out of hand. By the end of the first century, therefore, the ritualistic eucharist had been distinguished from the dinner party, and the fathers were universally agreed that its weekly celebration not only symbolized most effectively the unity of the church, but was also the most efficacious way in which this unity was actually brought about.

In baptism, as we have seen, one is 'incorporated' into the mystical body of Christ, but in the eucharist one is joined to Christ in a yet more intimate relationship. Not only does the shared meal symbolize the unity of the body of Christ and its members, but the body of Christ actually enters the believers and is made one with them. Communicants become (in the words of Cyril of Jerusalem) 'Christ-bearers,' and thereby share or participate in the divine nature. By taking Christ bodily within themselves, Christians are gradually transformed into Christ, and hence into God; and the eucharist was seen by both western and eastern fathers (but especially the latter) as the most important means of human 'deification' or 'divinization.' By the gradual transformation which is effected by the body and blood of Christ, Christians in turn become more truly the mystical body of Christ, and the church, thereby feeding on itself, becomes more truly what it actually is.

How the change from bread to body, or wine to blood, was actually brought about was not a matter of great concern to the fathers. They believed without question that a change did occur and, on the whole, did not care to speculate on the mechanism. The only notable exception is Gregory of Nyssa, and we should perhaps say a word about his theory, not because it is successful (one cannot, after all, explain the inexplicable), but because it is the only theory we have. Christ, says Gregory, ate and drank, and by the usual metabolic processes, what he ate and drank was slowly transformed into his body and blood. It is therefore possible to see in this process not a change from one thing X to another thing Y, utterly different and alien, but a transmutation of something which is *potentially* X to something which is *actually* X. Bread, for a human being, is potentially body; wine is potentially blood; so what happens in the eucharist is that by his divine power God transforms the potential into the actual, and does not perform a conjuring trick like changing a pocket handkerchief into a rabbit. And then, Gregory continues, the real flesh and blood of Christ is taken into ourselves and these fuse or meld or mix or blend (the Greek verb means all these things) with us, so that by sharing in Christ's immortality we, too, may become immortal.

The writers of the patristic period were also quite certain that the eucharist was a sacrifice. They qualify the term with such words as 'spiritual' sacrifice or 'bloodless' sacrifice, but they were in no doubt that when the body of Christ was offered up by the priest at the altar, it was a true reenactment of the sacrifice at Calvary. But there was obviously only one Calvary and there are many altars: are we then suggesting that there are many sacrifices and many bodies? No, said the fathers. Since Christ has only one body, there can be only one sacrifice. We always offer the same person; we always offer the same victim; we always offer the same oblation. John Chrysostom, bishop of Constantinople at the very end of the fourth century (he died in tragic circumstances in 407), is one of the clearest exponents of this idea, but he speaks not for himself but for all Christians. Furthermore, because there is but one sacrifice, and because that sacrifice is spiritually identical with the Calvary sacrifice, the effects of the Calvary sacrifice are also manifested in the eucharist. And since one of the most important effects of the crucifixion was the forgiveness of sins and the redemption of the world, so, too, in the eucharist these effects are reenacted, represented (in the literal sense: 're-presented,' 'presented once again'), and reapplied. The eucharistic sacrifice does not *add* to the Calvary sacrifice—that would be a blasphemous suggestion—but it continually 'realizes' it: continually makes it real and present.

On the other hand, the body of Christ is not only the bread on the altar, but also the church. It follows, then, as Augustine points out, that when the church offers up Christ in the eucharistic sacrifice it also offers up itself. It is not only the sacrifice of Christ, bringing with it redemption and remission of sins, but a self-sacrifice of all those individual Christians who are the members of his body. 'The whole redeemed community,' says Augustine,

> that is, the congregation and society of the saints, is offered to God as a universal sacrifice through the great Priest, who also offered himself in his Passion for us, so that we might be the body of such a great head. . . . This is the sacrifice of Christians—who are many, but one body in Christ [Rom 12:5]—which the church repeatedly celebrates in the sacrament of the altar, so familiar to the faithful. Here it is shown to [the church] that in what it offers, it is itself offered.[1]

This remarkable doctrine could almost turn one into a Christian. For there is no doubt that all these ideas may be combined together to produce a rich and impressive theory of the eucharist and its effects. By participation in this rite individual Christians assert their membership in the church and are mystically united with the body and blood of their risen Lord. By this uniting they share in the properties of that Lord: his immortality and his perfection, though the full realization of these is reserved for the life to

---

[1]Augustine of Hippo, *De civitate Dei* 10.6.

come. By participation in the eucharist, Christians 'incorporate' themselves into the body of Christ and are themselves 'impregnated' by the body into which they are incorporated. They become 'Christ-bearers,' and the Christ within them both demands and makes possible a more perfect and more Christian life. At the eucharist the historical event of Calvary—the one sufficient sacrifice, once offered— is transformed into an ever-present and ever-repeated reality, which, by its very nature, brings with it redemption and the remission of sins. And finally, in this comprehensive act, the church sacrifices itself to the Lord who sacrificed himself for it, and since eternal life is promised only to those who have no concern for their lives in this world (Jn 12:25), the eucharist is a pledge and guarantee of immortality.

Let us now, therefore, investigate where this immortality is to be enjoyed (or endured). What is the nature of heaven (and hell), and what dramatic events await us when we have shuffled off this mortal coil and have passed that bourn from which no traveller returns? What is the nature of the Christian's hope and the Christian's expectation?

THE BAPTISM OF CHRIST. Mosaic, fifth-century.

HARROWING HELL. Adapted from a fourteenth-century russian icon.

CHAPTER XVI

LAST THINGS

I T SEEMS FITTING, though predictable, that we should devote this last chapter to a discussion of the last things: those momentous events which will bring this world to its close and ourselves to judgment. The fathers were quite certain that three events would be involved: the Second Coming of Christ, a General Resurrection, and a Last Judgment, after which we would be justly consigned either to eternal bliss or eternal torment. But beyond a general acceptance of these three factors there was considerable disagreement as to where, when, and how these cataclysmic events would take place. Three questions in particular demand our attention: firstly, was there to be an interval between the Second Coming and the General Resurrection, and if so, how long was it to be? Secondly, what happened to individual souls in the period between the death of the body and the General Resurrection? And thirdly, what sort of body was it that arose at the sound of the last trumpet?

The twentieth chapter of the Book of Revelation is full of the idea of a thousand-year reign. Satan is bound for a thousand years; the martyrs reign with Christ for a thousand years; there is a cataclysm at the end of the thousand years. These ideas came over into Christianity from the messianic speculations of later Judaism, and they proved very popular during the first two centuries. Jesus would descend to earth—almost certainly in Jerusalem—and would then establish an earthly kingdom to last for a millenium. It would be a time of peace and plenty. The righteous would rise from the dead to enjoy it, and if we may believe Irenaeus of Lyons, food of every kind would be available in overwhelming abundance. Every grain of wheat would produce ten thousand ears; every ear would produce ten thousand grains; and every grain would produce ten pounds of the finest flour (if these are Roman pounds, by the way, this gives us nearly three hundred and thirty-five thousand tons of flour per grain of wheat: the righteous saints must have been up to their necks in it). All the animals will live in peace and harmony (this idea comes from Isaiah 11: even lions turn vegetarian), and all will be totally obedient. Certain heretical groups (like followers of Cerinthus, a Gnostic heretic who flourished at the end of the first century) went further than this and envisaged the millenium as a thousand years of indulgence in gluttony, lechery, drinking parties, and festivals. But this was not, emphatically not, the teaching of the Christian church.

These millenial ideas were widespread and popular, but despite the authority of such formidable figures as Irenaeus, Justin, Hippolytus, and Tertullian, Origen was not prepared to accept them at all. As an Alexandrian his approach was naturally much more allegorical, and he reinterpreted both the Second Coming and the millenium in a fully spiritual sense. He was well aware of the arguments in use and of the proof-texts cited, and knew that there were many who believed that the righteous saints would eat and drink and copulate in the New Jerusalem. But though these people believe in Christ, he says, they are interpreting the divine Scriptures in a Jewish way, and that is not fitting for Christians. Yes, the saints will eat—but they will eat the bread of life which feeds the soul and illuminates the mind with the food of wisdom and truth. Yes, they will drink—but from the cup of divine wisdom. And this food and drink will not serve to feed the body and satisfy the senses, but to restore the soul to the image and likeness of God.

The arguments of Origen were certainly persuasive, and they came at a time when there was a general and growing dissatisfaction with the more physical and materialistic interpretations of Christ's Second Coming; and although belief in the millenium lingered on in some places for a further century, it did so only as the view of a small and uninfluential minority. The majority view of the churches by Origen's time was that the General Resurrection would follow directly upon the Second Coming, and this naturally introduces the question of just what happens to an individual's soul immediately after physical death. Is it conscious or unconscious? Is it aware or unaware? Where does it go? Is it judged at that time as well as at the General Resurrection? And so on.

The Gnostics, on the whole, maintained that once the soul had been released from the body by death, it immediately began its ascent to heaven, and in opposition to this thesis the earlier writers—Irenaeus, for example—asserted the contrary. As Christ descended into hell for three days, so the souls of the departed enter an invisible underworld, 'the shadow of death,' marked out for them by God. There they must wait until the Resurrection, when they will receive back their bodies and arise complete and entire to be ushered into the presence of God. Tertullian is even more explicit: the underworld is a vast emptiness or a concealed abyss deep in the earth, and it is here that the souls of the dead await the Resurrection. So long as the earth remains intact, therefore, there is no way out of this deep pit, and only when the earth is shattered at the end of all things will the souls there imprisoned be released. But, says Tertullian, in this underworld there is both punishment and refreshment: a sort of anticipation of the eternal bliss or everlasting torment yet to come. It would be unjust, he says, if in that dark cavern the souls of the wicked prospered or the souls of the righteous were afflicted. So if we interpret 'the last penny' of Matthew 5:26 correctly, we find that it refers to 'every trifling transgression which must be expiated there in the period before the Resurrection.'[1]

This is clearly an anticipation of the later doctrine of purgatory. Tertullian does not here mention fire, that is true, and in another of his writings he seems to indicate that these little sins must be expiated during our life here and not hereafter, but despite his uncertainties, there is no doubt that he is beginning to think in purgatorial terms. Clement of Alexandria carries the idea further and maintains more specifically that if people repent on their deathbeds and therefore have no opportunity of performing penance here and now, they may be cleansed in the next life by purifying fire. There are some, says he, like the deaf adders of Psalm 58:4, who will not listen to the Lord's song. Let them be chastised, therefore, by God's fatherly admonitions *before* the final judgment, so that by being ashamed and repenting, they might not inherit eternal pain. Most of us, Clement continues, have deserved these chastisements, but even though we have fallen into sin, we are still of the Lord's people.

Nevertheless, despite the evidence that such ideas were in circulation, it would be premature to speak of 'the doctrine' of purgatory. There was just too much uncertainty surrounding the question of what happened to the soul immediately after death—particularly among the eastern theologians—and although in the west the ideas rapidly coalesced, it is not until after Augustine that we can begin to speak of 'the doctrine' of purgatory with any real meaning. But from the third century onwards it seems that

---

[1]Tertullian, *De anima* 58.

the Christian consensus was that the soul after death is not in a state of sleep, unconsciousness, or suspended animation, but awaits the final judgment with its senses intact, and that it probably anticipates this judgment with pain or with happiness. The pain may then serve to cleanse the soul of at least minor sins so that by the time of the judgment itself it may be presented before its Creator in as clean a condition as possible. Not until Jerome is this immediate foretaste referred to specifically as a 'judgment,' and not until the fourteenth century do we find it officially recognized as part of the doctrine of the church. At that time Pope Benedict XII denied any intermediate post-mortem state in which the souls of the departed 'anticipated' the future consequences of their earthly actions. Instead, he declared, there was an immediate judgment, and the souls of the dead went straightaway to heaven, hell, or purgatory. But even with papal authority behind it, there was still considerable medieval uncertainty over the matter, and the situation a thousand years earlier was that much more fluid. In any case, the biblical evidence itself is conflicting, for whereas some texts indicate without question that the General Resurrection, Second Coming, and Final Judgment were intimately related, the parable of Dives and Lazarus seemed to imply that there was an immediate and particular judgment following bodily death. Confusion and uncertainty were only to be expected, therefore, and although the idea of what we might call 'anticipated judgment' (which might or might not be purgatorial) was very widespread, it would be quite incorrect to refer to it as 'the doctrine' of the church. It was, however, the most widely circulated idea among a considerable number of ideas and speculations.

Despite the general acceptance of some sort of 'anticipated judgment,' none of the fathers ever denied the Final Judgment yet to come and, as a prelude to that awful event, the resurrection of the body. But what sort of body? The physical one we have now, with all its cuts, bruises, pimples, defects, warts, myopia, baldness, and haemorrhoids? Or a spiritual body (as St Paul suggests) in which all these things are transcended?

The earliest writers—the Apostolic Fathers and the Apologists—tended to the first of these two alternatives. Given the problems they had with Gnosticism this is quite understandable, for the Gnostics (as we saw in Chapter II) considered matter, flesh, and created stuff evil and utterly denied the possibility of solid flesh inhabiting the wholly transcendent kingdom of the Supreme Being. For them, resurrection was entirely spiritual, and the body was thankfully left behind to rot away in the earth. And the earth was welcome to it.

No, said the Christians, this is not the case at all. The resurrection of Christ anticipates our resurrection, and in the ascension of Christ, it was not just his soul that ascended into heaven, but his soul in its resurrected body. In any case, they said, God can do anything, and if he could make a human body with all its muscles and veins and bones and blood and life and rationality (this is Irenaeus of Lyons speaking), he would surely have no problem resurrecting this same body once it had returned to its constituent elements. Look at the seasons, says Tertullian: winter follows autumn, autumn follows summer, summer follows spring. The trees bare their branches and are reclothed in green; the flowers look dead, but then burst forth in glory! They all return after they have departed; they all begin again after they have faded away. 'Nothing perishes except to be restored, and the whole order of things . . . is a witness to the resurrection of the dead.'[2] In any case, if your flesh with all its idiosyncrasies does not rise, how can you be sure that God will recognize you? I have no objection to being accredited, by error, with other people's merits, but I have no desire to be saddled with their sins.

---

[2]Tertullian, *De resurrectione carnis* 12.

To this literal and materialistic interpretation of resurrection, the allegorical Origen strongly objected. This, by
now, should cause us no surprise. Yet he does not deny the
doctrine—to do so would be to deny a fundamental principle of the Christian tradition—but reinterprets it in a more
satisfactory sense. What he says (effectively) is that all
bodies are in a state of metabolic transformation and that
during the course of one's life the actual bodily stuff of
which one is made is in a state of unceasing change. Yet
despite this, an individual of twenty is, in a certain way,
the same individual at sixty and can be recognized as such.
This is because there is a bodily 'form' or 'shape' or 'appearance' which remains essentially constant while all else
changes. It is like the river of Heraclitus: the water in which
I am paddling now is not the same as it was ten seconds
ago. To that extent it is a totally different river. Yet I still
recognize it as the same stream. So when the saints rise
again, says Origen, they will retain the same form/shape/
appearance, but the substances which make up this form
will not be the fleshly ones, suitable for fleshly life on this
earth, but spiritual ones, suitable for spiritual life in
heaven. 'It is sown in corruption; it is raised in incorruption. It is sown in dishonour; it is raised in glory. It is sown
in weakness; it is raised in power. It is sown an animal
body; it is raised a spiritual body' (1 Cor 15:42–44).

This is a concept which, on the whole, may be more
satisfactory for most modern Christian believers, but it was
certainly not a concept which went unchallenged. Some
opponents pointed out that the physical form or appearance is the least constant thing about the body, and it is
certainly the thing that perishes first when death and damp
and worms take over. Others pointed to Christ's meeting
with doubting Thomas: if that disciple could actually put
his fingers in the holes left by the nails and the spear then it
must have been the same flesh which died on the cross.

Transfigured, perhaps, and transformed and spiritualized and resurrected and what have you: but basically and substantially the same flesh.

Such objections were not without force. If I make a statue of a particular person out of silver, melt it down, and then make a second statue of the same person out of gold, there is a sense in which it is not the same statue. What Origen's opponents wanted to do was to replace the idea of *substitution* (substituting spiritual matter for fleshly matter) with *spiritualization* or *transformation*. Here we make our statue from lead, and then God the Divine Alchemist, in ways known only to himself, *transforms* or *spiritualizes* the lead into gold. It is indeed the fleshly body which is raised, but by God's spiritualizing influence the resurrected flesh has certain properties which it does not at present possess. It will be immortal, for example, and no longer subject to corruption. If this were not so, how could the wicked burn for ever? The act of cremation is over in a comparatively short time, and if we do not have flesh which is eternally flammable, then we would be forced to resort to a punishment similar to that found in the Qur'ān: when one lot of skin has been burned away, God creates another lot so that the process can continue *ad infinitum* (Qur'ān 4:56).

Hard-line Origenists were therefore few (only Gregory of Nyssa really followed closely in his master's footsteps), and the general tendency in both east and west was to adapt the 'spiritualization' rather than the 'substitution' theory. Yet the west, typically, laid greater stress than did the east on the essential identity of the physical flesh with the resurrected flesh (Jerome, reacting against Origen, is particularly insistent on this), and Augustine stresses that when St Paul speaks of a 'spiritual' body, he does not mean that the flesh has been converted into spirit, but that the resurrected body will submit to the spirit 'with the greatest and most wonderful ease of obedience.' Yet he also admits that the new body will be incorruptible and immortal, and not only will it not be such as it is now when it is in perfect health, it will not even be such as it was in the first humans before sin. It will, instead, be better than both, and when Augustine denies the straightforward conversion of flesh into spirit, he is not denying a certain spiritualization of the fleshly elements.

For both east and west, then, the Second Coming heralded the resurrection of both good and bad, their appearance before the divine Judge in spiritualized-fleshly bodies, and their ultimate consignation to heaven or to hell. But what are these places like? What are their essential characteristics? What is the nature of the infernal torments or the inconceivable joys of Paradise?

Hell and its pains are fairly well described in the New Testament, though for imagination and ingenuity the biblical accounts cannot compare with the descriptions of later medieval writers. According to the Scriptures, it is a place of outer darkness, of weeping and gnashing of teeth, of ever-burning fire (with or without brimstone), and of the worm that dieth not. It is also unquestionably everlasting, and the few brave souls who questioned this revolting doctrine had no significant impact on the orthodox Christian tradition. For Origen, so frequently an odd man out, the idea of eternal torment was incompatible with the doctrine of a loving God who was perfectly good, with the all-important concept of human free-will, and with the Pauline statement that God will reign until he has put all his enemies under his feet (1 Cor 15:25). His view, therefore, was that after inconceivable cycles of time, all beings would achieve redemption, including Satan (the 'last enemy' of 1 Cor 15:26), and this optimistic doctrine was also the view of Origen's admirer, Gregory of Nyssa. It was not, however, the view of the remaining 99.99% of the Christian community, and despite occasional and momentary doubts from such stalwart guardians of orthodoxy as

Gregory of Nazianzus, the universal Christian opinion by the end of the fourth century was that the torment was as eternal as it was terrible.

It was also the opinion of the fathers that the infernal pains were physical, not psychological. Origen, inevitably, held the latter view, but hardly anyone else did. There were different degrees of torment since there are different degrees of sin, but it was an external pain applied to bodily limbs. The fire was real, material, and everlasting, and the only mitigation of this idea appears in the distinct though unformed ideas of purgatory we discussed above. This is particularly evident in western writers, and we find such notable authorities as Ambrose and Jerome proposing that while the wholly wicked will be tormented forever, 'Christian' sinners—those who have believed in Christ, but have erred and strayed in comparatively minor ways—will be purified by the fire and eventually saved. But as we said earlier, the western doctrine of purgatory was not formalized until after the time of Augustine, and the eastern churches—for reasons which we cannot discuss at present—were eventually to reject it altogether.

What, then, of heaven? Much of the physical imagery stems, of course, from the Book of Revelation. It is there that we find the New Jerusalem with its pearly gates (twelve of them), its streets of transparent gold, its towering walls (some 220 feet high), its square city plan (covering about two million square miles by my reckoning), the throne of God, the river, the tree of life, the crystal sea, the elders with their harps, and so on. But although these images may have been—and certainly still are —much caressed at the popular level (but at *which* of the twelve pearly gates does St. Peter stand? Many of the fathers held more refined ideas. The Alexandrian tradition, understandably, tended to think of heaven as the realm of the Platonic Ideas, of the perfect archetypes of the imperfect realities here below, to which was added the sublime vision or indescribable experience of the Divine Trinity itself.

It is this which is the Beatific Vision, the culmination of Christian endeavour, and for the eastern fathers it coincided with the completion of the process of deification. Gregory of Nyssa is particularly insistent on this point and tells us that not only will we participate in the divine immortality and incorruption, but in the divine perfection and glory as well. Our knowledge, so limited and fragmentary here below, is there expanded into God, and we shall contemplate and experience the vision of God, not through a glass darkly, in a riddle and an enigma, but face to face. It is a realm of supreme delight and supreme rest; of unsullied joy and uttermost bliss; of meetings with loved ones past and—as the western fathers especially stressed—with the confessors and martyrs and saints. But just as in hell, so, too, in heaven there are gradations; and some writers, though by no means all, suggested that even after living holy lives here on earth, the souls of the righteous in Paradise continue to make gradual progress, stage by stage, until they achieve final beatitude. These are the 'many mansions' of which Christ spoke in John's gospel (Jn 14:2), but the very end of our progress (says Augustine) is the happy realization that there is indeed no end. God is Insatiable Satiety (it is Augustine's expression), and anyone who sinks down into that trinitarian abyss goes on sinking further down forever.

These are not concepts we can at present comprehend. The eyes and the mind of the resurrection body are subtly spiritualized, says Augustine again, and are thereby enabled to see and conceive things wholly impossible for us now. The Beatific Vision is the supreme experience, the truest and fullest happiness ever to be attained, the realization of all our desires, and the culmination of the Christian hope. It is the endless Sabbath whose end (says Augustine, one last and final time) 'will not be an evening, but the Day of the Lord, a sort of eighth and eternal day, consecrated by the resurrection of Christ and prefiguring not only the eternal rest of the spirit, but that of the body as well. There we shall be still and we shall see; we shall see and we shall love; we shall love and we shall give praise. Behold what will be at the end without end! For what else is our end, but to attain the Kingdom which has no end?'[3]

---

[3]Augustine, *De civitate Dei* 22.30.5.

INDEX

CISTERCIAN PUBLICATIONS INC.

Kalamazoo, Michigan

TITLES LISTING

THE CISTERCIAN FATHERS SERIES

THE WORKS OF BERNARD OF CLAIRVAUX

THE WORKS OF WILLIAM OF SAINT THIERRY

Texts and Studies
in the
Monastic Tradition

THE WORKS OF AELRED OF RIEVAULX

THE WORKS OF GILBERT OF HOYLAND

THE WORKS OF JOHN OF FORD

OTHER EARLY CISTERCIAN WRITERS

* Temporarily out of print

† Forthcoming

THE CISTERCIAN STUDIES SERIES

MONASTIC TEXTS

CHRISTIAN SPIRITUALITY

MONASTIC STUDIES

CISTERCIAN STUDIES

* *Temporarily out of print*   † *Forthcoming*

* *Temporarily out of print*   † *Forthcoming*

Saint Gregory Nazianzen: Selected Poems

Eight Chapters on Perfection and Angel's Song
(Walter Hilton)

Creative Suffering (Iulia de Beausobre)

Bringing Forth Christ. Five Feasts of the Child
Jesus (St Bonaventure)

Gentleness in St John of the Cross

Distributed in North America only for Fairacres Press.

DISTRIBUTED BOOKS

St Benedict: Man with An Idea (Melbourne Studies)

The Spirit of Simplicity

Benedict's Disciples (David Hugh Farmer)

The Emperor's Monk: A Contemporary Life of
Benedict of Aniane

A Guide to Cistercian Scholarship (2nd ed.)

*North American customers may order
through booksellers or directly from
the publisher:*

Cistercian Publications
St Joseph's Abbey
Spencer, Massachusetts 01562
(508) 885–7011

*Cistercian Publications are available
in Britain, Europe and the Common-
wealth through A. R. Mowbray &
Co Ltd   St Thomas House   Oxford
OX1 1SJ.
For a sterling price list, please consult
Mowbray's General Catalogue.*

*A complete catalogue of texts-in-
translation and studies on early,
medieval, and modern Christian
monasticism is available at no
cost from Cistercian Publications.*

*Cistercian monks and nuns have been
living lives of prayer & praise, meditation
& manual labor since the twelfth century.
They are part of an unbroken tradition
which extends back to the fourth century
and which continues today in the Catholic
church, the Orthodox churches, the
Anglican communion, and most recently,
in the Protestant churches.*

*Share their way of life and their search for
God by reading Cistercian Publications.*

Cistercian Publications
Editorial Offices
WMU Station
Kalamazoo, Michigan 49008
(616) 387–5090

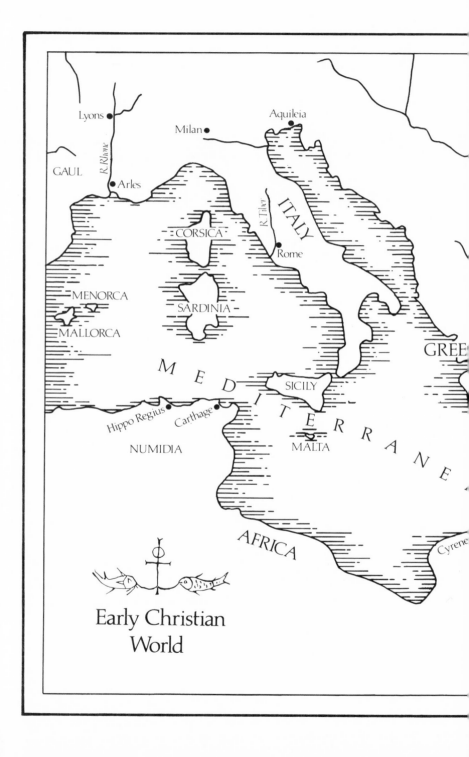

Early Christian
World

N.